ERIC GILL : SCULPTURE

ERIC GILL : SCULPTURE

Judith Collins

Lund Humphries, London
in association with Barbican Art Gallery
1992

Facing title,
previous page:
La Belle Sauvage 1932
cat.91

First edition 1992
Published by
Lund Humphries Publishers Ltd
Park House, 1 Russell Gardens,
London NW11 9NN
in association with
Barbican Art Gallery, London

British Library Cataloguing in Publication Data:
A catalogue record for this book is available from
the British Library
ISBN 0 85331 629 5

This catalogue accompanies the exhibition
Eric Gill: Sculpture
organised by Barbican Art Gallery, London

Exhibition tour:
Barbican Art Gallery, London:
11 November 1992 – 7 February 1993
Oriel 31, Newtown, Powys:
27 February – 4 April 1993
Leeds City Art Gallery
late April – late June 1993

Exhibition selected by
Judith Collins

Exhibition organised by
John Hoole, Donna Loveday, Tomoko Sato

Catalogue edited by
Judith Collins, John Hoole, Donna Loveday,
Lucy Myers, Tomoko Sato

Designed by Richard Hollis

Made and printed in Great Britain by
BAS Printers Limited, Over Wallop,
Hampshire

Contents

Model for Sculpture:
Ariel Piping to the Children 1931
cat.87

Foreword

The preparation of this exhibition has been a voyage of discovery for me. I have long admired the work of Eric Gill as a graphic designer and it is no coincidence that Gill Sans is the font that this gallery uses in its logo. Yet, working alongside the exhibition selector, Dr Judith Collins, I have gradually had revealed to me a side of the artist that has remained overlooked or hidden since his death in 1940.

¶ Over the last fifty years his reputation as a pioneering modernist designer has become consolidated but his renown as a monumental stone-mason, outspoken Catholic campaigner and an anti-capitalist critic has been largely forgotten. The recent biography by Fiona MacCarthy has revived interest in his life and art; this exhibition now offers a unique opportunity to see a fine selection of his most substantial and yet most inaccessible works. Because of their very nature, some very large, some immovable, his sculptures are difficult to congregate and, with many of his best smaller sculpture held in American library collections, and his largest works fixed to public buildings, this exhibition provides the first occasion for nearly fifty sculptures and many more related studies to be seen together.

¶ Recent studies about Gill have tried to analyse or reconcile his public and private faces. I think that viewers of Gill's work will have to grapple with the notion proposed by George Orwell in his essay on Salvador Dali, that an artist's work can be brilliant and, at the same time, the individual's manner very demanding, without the one diminishing the other. On Dali's art and his psychological make-up, Orwell advocated diagnosis. 'The question is not so much *what* he is as *why* he is like that.'[1] Judith Collins has tried in this publication to provide a detailed description and analysis of his sculpture and I have no doubt that this will lead to a greater understanding and appreciation of Gill's greatest achievements.

¶ To enable this exhibition to happen, we are indebted to a variety of lenders and supporters, without whose assistance we would not have been able to succeed. In particular, we would like to thank Dr Thomas Staley and his staff at the Harry Ransom Humanities Research Center, The University of Texas at Austin; Derek Pullen

1. *George Orwell: Collected Essays*, Mercury Books 1961, p.215. I am indebted to Judy Digney for this reference.

and Jackie Heuman of the Sculpture Conservation Studio at the Tate Gallery, Keith Taylor of Taylor Pearce Restoration Services Ltd, and John Dennis of the Dallas Museum of Art, who all contributed to the cleaning programme; John Skelton and Dr Terry Friedman at the Henry Moore Centre for the Study of Sculpture, Leeds, for their generous loans of photographs; and, finally to Valmai Ward and the Welsh Arts Council and to Momart Ltd for the careful handling of the exhibits.

¶ Finally, I would like to join with Judith Collins in offering special thanks to Sir Alan Bowness, the Director of The Henry Moore Foundation, who has provided continued encouragement and assistance for this project.

John Hoole
Curator
Barbican Art Gallery

Preface

This is the first exhibition to attempt a retrospective of the figurative sculpture of Eric Gill. His career as a sculptor spanned the years 1910 to 1940; the exhibition is however stronger in work of the years between 1910 and 1930 than that of the 1930s, because by then, Gill's growing fame led to many public commissions, which being architectural in context, have had to remain *in situ*. These include the London Underground Headquarters sculptures at St James's Park, London, and the sculptures for Broadcasting House. It is surprising how many sculptures by Gill, well documented at the time of their execution, have since vanished without trace. It would be a bonus if this exhibition began to bring them forth from their hiding places. It would also be a bonus if this exhibition initiated a thorough study of the sculptural output of Gill, with due accord given to his formal inventiveness, technical excellence and unusual subject-matter, over and above that of his well-researched life style.

¶ Many people and institutions have helped this exhibition become a reality and I am pleased to be able to acknowledge their generous support. Foremost among them have been Sir Alan Bowness and The Henry Moore Foundation, who supplied the means for me to undertake initial research of the Gill sculpture holdings in California and Texas. The staff at the Harry Ransom Humanities Research Center, The University of Texas at Austin were especially cooperative, particularly Dr Thomas Staley, Sue Murphy and Kathleen Gee. I am sorry that legal constraints prevent any loans from the William Andrews Clark Memorial Library in Los Angeles, because there are fine Gill sculptures there, which are destined to remain unseen except by the library users. The following people have also been most helpful: Victor Arwas; Tony Bradshaw of The Bloomsbury Workshop; Ivor Braka; Bernard and Judith Bumpus; Tom Craig; Sir Roger Cary; David Collins, Faustus Fine Art; Sir Brinsley Ford; Janet Green, Sotheby's; Anne Goodchild, Graves Art Gallery, Sheffield; Jackie Heuman, Tate Gallery; Elsbeth Lindner; Sandra Lummis; Gillian and Neville Jason; Brian Keeble; Rev. Graham Kent; Timothy McCann, West Sussex Record Office, Chichester; Fiona MacCarthy; Sandra Martin, Manchester City Art

Galleries; James Mosley, St Bride Printing Library; David Peace; Derek Pullen, Tate Gallery; Jennifer Rennie, City Museum and Art Gallery, Stoke-on-Trent; R. Rhodes, Headmaster, Rossall School; John and Myrtle Skelton; Peyton Skipwith; Susan Slade; Timothy Wilcox, Hove Museum and Art Gallery.
¶ Finally I would like to thank Michael Nixon of Oriel 31, Newtown, and Dr Terry Friedman of the Henry Moore Centre for the Study of Sculpture, Leeds City Art Gallery, for fruitful discussions about Gill, which have brought us all this far.

Judith Collins

League of Nations Creation Relief (detail) 1935
see cat.100

THE SCULPTURE OF ERIC GILL

There has, until now, been no attempt to survey Eric Gill's œuvre as a sculptor. His thousand wood engravings have been reproduced in facsimile and his 762 lettered inscriptions listed; a bibliography reveals the 550 articles he wrote for publication, as well as the numerous books he illustrated. He also designed several typefaces, still in use today. He was a prolific speaker and writer on artistic, social and theological topics. Taken together all these strands build a picture of an extremely busy man, which his meticulously kept diaries and worksheets confirm. However, the core of his output and the thing that took up most of his time was the act of carving stone. His chosen epitaph on his headstone was as 'Eric Gill, Stone Carver', and in his engraved self-portrait he wears a stone-mason's paper hat. Gill probably carved about 500 stone sculptures, many of which take their place as part of an architectural scheme. Some are familiar landmarks in British towns and cities, especially the war memorials at Chirk, North Wales, and Trumpington, near Cambridge. The time is ripe for an assessment of Gill's sculptural achievement and this exhibition and catalogue hope to initiate that process.

¶ Gill occupies a unique place in British sculptural life of the twentieth century. He was born on 22 February 1882 in Brighton, the eldest son of twelve children of Arthur Tidman and Rose Gill. Eric Gill described his father as 'an Anglican parson, formerly a Dissenter', and his grandfather and great-uncle were Congregationalist missionaries in the South Sea Islands. The strong sense of vocation displayed by these three close male relatives was inherited by Gill, who appeared to feel from early manhood that he had a divinely appointed task to do. This task was to communicate his vision of art as a vehicle for the splendours of spiritual life. And in order to do this, Gill began to produce figurative sculpture that was uncompromising in its sacred message.

¶ His father, Arthur Tidman Gill, separated himself from the established Anglican Church for a period in order to examine his beliefs, and Gill followed in like manner. The final section of Gill's *Autobiography* is entitled 'Escapades' and in this he listed the seven establishments or systems of thought from which he extricated himself in order to find his own unique path. The seven escapes were from the art school in Chichester; the architectural profession; scientific materialism; the Arts and Crafts Movement; Socialism; London; and the Fine Art world, and they occurred between the years 1897 and *circa* 1913.

1. A Sure Foundation

In 1897 Gill became a student at Chichester Technical and Art School, where it was assumed he would train to be an art-master. There he gained an ability to copy nature, to produce perspectival drawings and decorative lettering, but also a disinclination to become an art-master. In 1900 Gill signed on to train to be an architect in the London office of William D. Caröe, who was employed as architect to the Ecclesiastical Commissioners. During his three years as an apprentice, from 1900 to 1903, Gill was supposed to attend evening lectures in the history of architecture. Instead he chose to spend his evenings studying the craft of monumental masonry at the Westminster Technical Institute, and writing and lettering under the inspirational Edward Johnston, at the Central School of Arts and Crafts. Gill began to obtain commissions for lettered inscriptions and he had to execute these in the evenings. In 1903, after receiving a large and important commission from the architect Edward Prior to cut inscriptions on the new Medical Schools that Prior was then building at Cambridge, Gill decided to leave the security of Caröe's office for the life of a self-employed craftsman. 'It was providential good fortune that I was able to do letter-cutting. I managed to hit on something which no one else was doing and which quite a lot of people wanted.'[1]
¶ In 1902, during an evening's lettering class, Johnston invited Gill to share his set of rooms at Lincoln's Inn, one of the four Inns of Court in London, and Gill moved from rented rooms in Clapham to Johnston's rooms in a handsome sixteenth-century building – '"Light's abode, celestial Salem" – I know it must seem absurd, but it was no less than heaven to me'.[2] Lincoln's Inn had courtyards, boundary walls and a locked gate each evening, and seemed to Gill to offer a semblance of collegiate or monastic life. It was his first taste of community life and work and it was one that deeply influenced the way he chose to live and work from then on. At Lincoln's Inn Gill discovered 'that neighbourliness need not mean only loving-kindness and readiness to lend a hand or a hammer; it

1. *Autobiography*, p.117

2. *Autobiography*, p.126

might also mean *unanimity*, an agreement in the mind as to the good and the true and the beautiful and a common practice founded thereon'.[3] The common agreement between neighbours that Gill cherished and wished to promote was one built upon spiritual foundations. Gill had likened Lincoln's Inn to a monastery and from about 1903 onwards, the time that he began to live the life of a professional letter-cutter, he began to work not only for himself, but also 'to please God'.

¶ When Edward Johnston married in 1904, Gill lived on for a short while in Johnston's rooms in Lincoln's Inn, and then with his own marriage to Ethel Moore that same year, moved to workmen's lodgings in Battersea. His career as a letter-cutter was thriving and he felt it was time to take stock of his position in life: 'having made some beginnings in the job of discovering a reasonable basis for lettering, the next thing was to discover the basis of a reasonable workshop life, a reasonable life for workmen'.[4] When he had first arrived in London, Gill had been interested in the cause of Socialism as promoted by John Ruskin and William Morris: 'my socialism was from the beginning a revolt against the intellectual degradation of the factory hands and the damned ugliness of all that capitalist-industrialism produced'.[5] Gill came to believe passionately that things had gone wrong with the advent of the Industrial Revolution, and the introduction of inhuman machine production of buildings, clothing, furniture, food and utensils. In the centuries prior to the Industrial Revolution,

there was no special thing called art. Art was making in general and anyone who made anything would, if the word had existed, have been called an artist. Art was simply the way of men with things; it was human work . . . Even the philosophers who, like St Thomas Aquinas, wrote and thought about everything under the sun, did not write or think about art as a special subject, a thing practised by some people and not others.[6]

The Industrial Revolution brought about a division in human society whereby the artist and the workman became separated. They had originally been one and the same person. That person made an object from its inception through to its completion, by their own labour, by the effort of their mental will and their physical strength. Gill believed that the object had a rightness and a beauty because the path from its conception in the mind of its maker and its resultant execution was by the same person's hands.

3. *Autobiography*, p.129

4. *Autobiography*, p.139

5. *Autobiography*, p.111

6. *Art and a Changing Civilisation*, London, John Lane The Bodley Head, 1934, p.123

Gill sketching in Rome 1906

16

'Production by machinery has produced the artist who is simply a designer. Every kind of work requires a designer because every kind of thing made is a thing made first of all in the imagination and someone must draw it out. But equally obviously, before industrialism, the business of design was commonly the business of the workman who actually made things. Now the designer is an entirely different person and one who needs not actually make anything but a drawing.'[7]

¶ Gill and the art critic Herbert Read had an exchange of letters in the mid-1930s about the personal and impersonal in art, and Gill reminded Read of the 'corner stone of my aesthetic' which was a child's statement: 'First I think and then I draw my think'. Gill believed that the simplicity and rightness of that aesthetic was endangered by the introduction of machinery, and that 'the government of manufacture by men of business instead of by tradesmen [meant] the immediate destruction of the essence of the thing called art. The idea of the artist is "formative of things and not formed by them". The form and the content are inseparable.'[8] When Gill began to make figure sculpture in 1909, he wrote that it was like 'A new alphabet – the word was made flesh'.[9] Gill made the analogy that he was converting a set of abstract symbols, letters, into material substance and by doing so was effecting an incarnation. Gill's younger brother, Cecil, confirmed this: 'All his work, his way of life, and his thought proceeded from his acceptance of the doctrine that the "word became flesh". I emphasize this because one cannot begin to understand Eric, or his life, his work, and his teaching, without understanding, even if not wholly accepting, this deep spring of his being: the incarnation of Jesus Christ.'[10] The quotation 'the word became flesh' comes from the beginning of the Gospel according to St John, and makes reference to the way God communicates with men. According to Christian belief, prior to the arrival on earth of Jesus Christ, God spoke to men through prophets. When God chose to send His Son in material form, Jesus was able to communicate directly with men without any medium in between. Gill began as a figurative sculptor using the method of direct carving, that is, the sculptor takes a piece of stone and without recourse to a clay model or the labour of another craftsman carves his conception straight out of the block. There is no intermediary between the original idea, 'the think', and the final formal statement in stone, and Gill was probably the first sculptor in England to work in this manner since medieval times.

7. *Art and a Changing Civilisation*, p.121

8. Ibid, p.77

9. *Autobiography*, p.159

10. Cecil Gill, 'Reminiscences', in Cecil Gill, Beatrice Warde and David Kindersley, *The Life and Works of Eric Gill*, William Andrews Clark Memorial Library, Los Angeles, 1968, pp.1–2

2. Ananda Coomaraswamy

An entry in Gill's diary for 10 January 1908 records that he attended a lecture at the Art Workers' Guild, London, given by Dr Ananda Coomaraswamy on Indian Art. Gill added the accompanying phrase 'a most splendid paper'. This appears to be the first time that Gill became aware of Coomaraswamy, and it seems he was immediately impressed by the man and his knowledge. At the end of his life, Gill wrote in his *Autobiography*:

There was one person . . . to whose influence I am deeply grateful; I mean the philosopher and theologian, Ananda Coomaraswamy. Others have written the truth about life and religion and man's work . . . Others have understood the true significance of erotic drawings and sculptures. Others have seen the relationships of the true and the good and the beautiful. Others have had apparently unlimited learning. Others have loved; others have been kind and generous. But I know of no one else in whom all these gifts and all these powers have been combined. I dare not confess myself his disciple; that would only embarrass him. I can only say that I believe that no other living writer has written the truth in matters of art and life and religion and piety with such wisdom and understanding.[11]

¶ Coomaraswamy was born in 1877 in Ceylon of a Tamil father and an English mother. He studied botany and geology at London University. The Home Office in London appointed Coomaraswamy Director of the first mineralogical survey of Ceylon from 1903 to 1906, and after completing this work, he travelled for the first time to India at the end of 1906. His time in Ceylon and India stimulated an abiding interest in the arts and crafts of those countries and their spiritual basis. In 1907 Coomaraswamy moved into a medieval building, the Norman Chapel at Broad Campden, restored for him by C. R. Ashbee who lived and worked a couple of miles away, at Chipping Campden.
¶ Ashbee had formed his Guild of Handicraft, a group of workers occupied in the arts and crafts, in the East End of London in 1888. In 1902 he took his ideas and his workers to Chipping Campden, an attractive and neglected Gloucestershire village, in order to test his theory that a rural life was better for the production of art and craft work than an urban one. Ashbee looked at the position of the worker and his occupation in the arts and crafts world, such as

11. *Autobiography*, p.174

silversmithing or printing, in terms of the social well-being of the individual and of society as a whole. Coomaraswamy allied himself to Ashbee's ideas and ideals, but substituted the spiritual for the social. Coomaraswamy purchased William Morris's press and used it to publish in 1908 the first book on the arts of his native Ceylon, *Medieval Sinhalese Art*. This was followed by *The Indian Craftsman* in 1909, *Indian Drawings* in 1910, and several articles in the *Burlington Magazine* between 1910 and 1916 on Indian art, later published in book form as *Rajput Painting* and *The Dance of Shiva*, the latter reviewed by Gill. In 1917 Coomaraswamy left Britain to take up a post as Keeper of the Indian Collections at the Museum of Fine Arts in Boston, a position he held until his death in 1947.

¶ Coomaraswamy was important for Gill for two reasons: firstly because he examined the relationship between man's work and his leisure, and secondly because he examined the relationship between the sacred and the profane. Also he provided Gill with a phrase that virtually became Gill's motto, and is thought by many to have stemmed from Gill himself, so perfectly does it chime with his aesthetic – 'The artist is not a special kind of man, but every man is a special kind of artist'. Gill was able to test his own Christian-based ideas against those of a Hindu, and thus gain a broader spiritual base, although many ideas were held in common. Coomaraswamy was looking for a new metaphysical system for man's work and life at just the same time that Gill was, but Coomaraswamy's aesthetic parameters were much wider. He offered a deep and first-hand knowledge of Indian and Ceylonese arts and crafts to a British audience anxious to learn more. And Gill was in the forefront of those thirsty for this knowledge.

¶ An appreciation in Britain of Indian arts and crafts emerged in the late 1870s, spearheaded by the artists William Morris, Edward Burne-Jones, John Everett Millais and Walter Crane. These men were only too aware of how the arts and crafts in Britain were being attacked by increasing industrialisation and they wished to focus attention on the same position occurring in India. From 1908 Coomaraswamy took up this cause with passion. Then in the Spring of 1910 the India Society was founded, with its headquarters in London. Among the founding members were Coomaraswamy, Walter Crane, W. R. Lethaby, Roger Fry and William Rothenstein, all of whom were colleagues of Gill and significant supporters of his emergent sculptural practice.

¶ In 1908 Coomaraswamy published *The Aims of Indian Art* and in this book cited William Blake as a most significant example of a Western artist who worked in an imaginative rather than a naturalistic manner. This way of thinking and working allied Blake to the aesthetics of Oriental artists. Blake was for Coomaraswamy a great and original spiritual thinker and artist and assumed for him the role of a bridge between Eastern and Western art. It is not inconceivable to imagine that Gill wanted to inherit Blake's role. In 1910 Gill designed a tombstone based on one of Blake's illustrations to Robert Blair's poem 'The Grave', the dramatic composition of 'The Reunion of the Soul and the Body'. And in 1917 Gill based his wood engraving of *The Last Judgement* on Blake's colour print of *God Judging Adam*. Gill, like Blake, believed in social and spiritual reform, and sexual freedom. They both abhorred the negative power of industrial mechanisation.

3. The Beginnings of Figural Sculpture

'My first erotic drawing was not on the back of an envelope but a week or so's work on a decent piece of hard stone.'[12] This was how Gill described his first essay into figural sculpture. Late in 1909 he carved a small relief of a crouching naked woman acting as a caryatid for a tablet bearing a Greek inscription, beginning with the words 'Estin Thalassa' (see *cat.1*). He remembered how excit-

Estin Thalassa 1909
Present whereabouts unknown
see cat.1

12. *Autobiography*,
p.158

ing this experiment was to him: 'I was responsible for her very existence and her every form came straight out of my heart'.[13] His erotic impulse, which was known to be very strong, had to endure abstinence at the end of 1909 when his wife Ethel was heavily pregnant with their third child, Joanna, who was born on 1 February 1910. In order to compensate for this abstinence, Gill carved himself this small substitute, on an oddly shaped piece of stone. It is significant that the impulse which drove Gill to take up drawing and carving in stone was sexual in origin. As he wrote: 'A new world opened before me . . . A new alphabet – the word was made flesh.'

¶ The lettered tablet which the naked woman supports has four lines of Greek, which are taken from Aeschylus' *Agamemnon*, line 959. Clytemnestra replies to her husband Agamemnon when he returns from the Trojan War that 'There is the sea, and who shall drain her dry'. He had rebuked her for extravagance in the use of purple dye to mark his return, and she had replied thus. Gill was fond of reading Greek literature in translation, but how and why he plucked out this single line and allied it to his naked female caryatid will probably never be answered. He sent the relief to a mixed exhibition at the Whitechapel Art Gallery, London, in May 1910, describing it as 'Tablet for the wall of a seaside house'. Perhaps memories of the sea from his childhood in Brighton had given this line special meaning for Gill.

¶ By the time that *Estin Thalassa* was on show at the Whitechapel Art Gallery, in a mixed exhibition which included some of the avant-garde artists then working in London, such as Jacob Epstein, Gill had embarked upon four or five further stone carvings. He had been inspired to do so partly because of the great enthusiasm for his first pieces shown by his friend, the painter William Rothenstein. Gill had shown the *Estin Thalassa* relief and a small group of a mother and child (*cat.2*) to Rothenstein very early in 1910. Rothenstein recalled how he

thought them admirable, and at once bought the mother and child. I thought [Count] Kessler would be interested and showed him the stone carvings; he at once acquired the second piece [Estin Thalassa]. Berenson, too, who was in London, asked Gill for a replica of the mother and child, and Gill thenceforth, while going on with his inscription carving, turned more and more to figure carving.[14]

¶ Gill made three small groups of a mother and child during 1910

13. *Autobiography*, p.159

14. Robert Speaight, unpublished Notebook 2 with transcripts from William Rothenstein's papers in the collection of Harvard University, National Art Library, p.28

and when the three were shown in Gill's first exhibition at the Chenil Gallery, Chelsea, in January 1911, the *Times* critic decided that Gill had tried to 'express the instinct of maternity' in a way that was 'animal and pathetic, not triumphant' and with 'a beauty which comes from the simplicity and force of the expression'. Critics focussed on the primitive, archaic quality of Gill's mother and child groups, and drew a comparison between Gill's approach and that of the Post-Impressionist painters, most notably Gauguin, whose paintings had just been on show in Roger Fry's first Post-Impressionist Exhibition. Fry wrote a review of Gill's Chenil Gallery show and made some important points about Gill's outlook and motivation.

¶ Fry stated that Gill was a sculptor 'to whom the language of plastic imagery is instinctive and natural' and

One realises before Mr Gill's simple, sincere and deeply-felt images what a profanation is the teaching of art as it is usually understood; the teaching, as dead facts, of that which each student should discover for himself as the result of an imperious need for expression. We can see Mr Gill finding out about the structure of the figure, and each discovery is given to us, not as a fact, but as a vividly apprehended emotional experience. And, owing to his technical skill, each discovery is rendered with unhesitating certainty and power. The result is that these

Mother and Child 1910
see cat.2

*figures are not more or less successful copies of that desperately unreal
and fictitious thing, the model posing in the studio, but positive crea-
tions, the outcome of a desire to express something felt in the adventure
of human life. And Mr Gill, having a religious faith in the value and
significance of life, has said what he thinks . . .*[15]

¶ Fry's ideas about Gill conform very well to Gill's own standpoint,
and this is not surprising since they were good friends at this point
in time, discussing questions about artistic expression and the role
of the artist in society. In December 1910 Fry wrote to Gill about
the work of the French Post-Impressionist painters whom he
admired and then continued:

*What a queer world it is but you have made it very exciting and more
full of hope for the future than I had dreamed say ten years ago. Then
I was mainly interested in myself, a completely dull subject and now
I suppose it's what you call God.*[16]

¶ Besides the *Mother and Child* groups at the Chenil Gallery exhibition, Gill showed two large stone figural reliefs which drew wide
attention and acclaim. These were *Crucifixion* (cat.6) and *A Roland
for an Oliver* (cat.4). They were hung side by side, and therefore
were meant to be seen as a pair. Indeed the title 'A Roland for an
Oliver' is another way of saying 'tit for tat' or an equally matched
contest. Gill's working titles for them were '*Schmerz*' for the
Crucifixion and '*Joie*' for the other. Both have lettered inscriptions
as part of their compositions and these texts help in the decipher-
ment of the complex meanings of this pair of reliefs. The *Crucifixion*
panel has incised Latin letters set vertically in the upright shaft of
the cross. These are taken from Psalm 147, v.10 and read 'He taketh
not delight in the legs of a man . . .'. The raised Greek letters set
out horizontally on either side of the cross are taken from the
Gospel of St Matthew, 19, v.12 and read '. . . and there be eunuchs,
which have made themselves eunuchs for the kingdom of heaven's
sake. He that is able to receive it [this saying], let him receive it.'
¶ Both biblical texts lay stress on the renunciation of the flesh,
which leads to an acknowledgement of the power of the spirit. The
figure of Christ has weak legs which fit well with the words from
the Psalm, and although He is displayed nude, His genitals are small.
Gill's Christ has accepted His sacrificial role and by His love has
renounced the physical world and all its attendant desires. The
other relief, *A Roland for an Oliver*, presents, as Fry described, a

15. Roger Fry, 'An English
Sculptor', *The Nation*, 28
January 1911, p.719

16. Letter, Gill Collection,
William Andrews Clark
Memorial Library, Los
Angeles

naked woman 'in all the insolent splendour, not indeed of her beauty, but of her unquenchable will to live'. The lettered inscription set into the raised frame of this relief is taken from lines 35 and 23–4 of Algernon Swinburne's 'Hymn to Proserpine', a poem which was included in his controversial book *Poems and Ballads*, published in 1866. Swinburne's book caused controversy in Victorian literary circles because of its uncompromising support for masochism and the attraction of *femmes fatales*, along with its outspoken repudiation of Christianity. The inscription on Gill's relief reads 'O pale Galilean But these/thou shalt not take the laurel/the palm and the paean the/breasts of the nymphs in the brake'. Swinburne's 'pale Galilean' is a reference to Christ, and in fact is a term first used by Julian the Apostate, a fourth-century Roman emperor who sought to denigrate Christianity and promote paganism by every means possible, a figure obviously admired by Swinburne.

¶ It seems, from what we know of Gill, that he had no intention of repudiating Christ in favour of sensual pagan rituals but he used these two reliefs to show that following the religious path in Edwardian England implied that if you chose Christ you had to reject the attractions of the 'breasts of the nymphs in the brake' and vice versa. Gill wanted to state his belief that it was possible to choose both paths simultaneously. One did not cancel the other out: on the contrary, they enhanced one another. The complementary poses of the two figures could be seen to bear this out. Gill's belief that the ascetic and the sensual could be amalgamated stemmed from his burgeoning knowledge of Indian art and Hindu theology.

¶ In 1913 Coomaraswamy published his *The Arts and Crafts of India and Ceylon* and a section of his chapter on Indian sculpture provides a most useful gloss on these two reliefs. Coomaraswamy had been describing how sculptures of spiritual figures were made more impressive if they were created in a voluptuous style:

. . . *in the best of Gothic art there are traces of a conflict, a duality of soul and body. If in many works of ancient Greece there is no such conflict, this is because the body alone is presented: but in the best of the Indian sculpture flesh and spirit are inseparable . . . In nearly all Indian art there runs a vein of deep sex-mysticism. Not merely are female forms felt to be equally appropriate with male to adumbrate the majesty of the Over-soul, but the interplay of all psychic and physical sexual forces is felt in itself to be religious. Already we find in one of the earliest Upanishads – 'For just as one who dallies with a beloved wife has no consciousness of outer and inner, so the spirit also, dallying with the Self-whose-essence-is-knowledge, has no consciousness of outer and inner'. Here is no thought that passion is degrading . . . but a frank recognition of the close analogy between amorous and religious ecstasy . . . It is thus that the imager, speaking always for the race, rather than of personal idiosyncracies, set side by side on his cathedral walls the yogi and the apsara, the saint and the ideal courtesan.[17]*

¶ Coomaraswamy's description of the imager setting his two works of the saint and courtesan side by side on a wall is virtually a description of what was on display in Gill's exhibition. The very full critical response to Gill's exhibition indicates that his impassioned message, made public here for the first time, was in no danger of being ignored, even if it was not yet time for it to be assimilated into current aesthetic and ethical thinking.

¶ A preparatory drawing exists for the relief *A Roland for an Oliver* (*cat.5*) and the body is drawn with greater confidence than the head. It looks as though Gill used a variety of sources and synthesised them together. There may have been some drawing from life; his diaries at this time indicate that female members of his family posed occasionally. But the face has the look of being copied from an illustration of archaic Greek sculpture. No preparatory drawing is known to exist for the *Crucifixion* panel, although there is an interesting source for the figure of Christ. On the back of a photograph of this relief,[18] in an unknown hand, is the message: 'EG 1910 Early work inspired by Gauguin's *Christ jaune*'. Gauguin was represented by forty-six works in Roger Fry's first Post-Impressionist Exhibition, although the *Christ jaune* was not one of these. Gill went round the exhibition with Fry. Gill does not give his opinion on Post-Impressionist painters such as Gauguin and Cézanne until much later. In 'Songs without clothes' in *Art-Nonsense and Other Essays*, published in 1929, Gill cites those kinds of art which have been offered up as praise to God. Following on from the primitive sculptures and paintings of India, China and Greece, he concludes with:

the works of those who, called 'Post-Impressionists', coming after that last dying flare of the idolaters, Impressionism, refusing to continue man's song of praise of himself, now dare again to utter absolute statements, and, however waywardly, and with whatever youthful flouting of your materialist and hedonist prejudices,

17. Ananda Coomaraswamy, *The Arts and Crafts of India and Ceylon*, pp.63–4

18. Gill Collection, Harry Ransom Humanities Research Center, The University of Texas at Austin

again say in paint and stone: Blessed by God; blessed by his holy Name.[19]

¶ Following earlier examples of his lettered inscriptions, Gill painted the incised Latin letters on the *Crucifixion* relief black and the full stops red. With *A Roland for an Oliver*, Gill decorated his pagan voluptuous woman by gilding her necklace and painting her lips and nipples red. *The Observer* noted that 'the gold chain round the woman's neck produces an effect dangerously near that of the black stockings in some of Felicien Rops' pornographic etchings'. Indeed, although both reliefs were greatly admired, and purchased from the exhibition by Roger Fry and Robert Ross for the newly formed Contemporary Art Society, there was general difficulty over the painted decorations which adorned the woman's body. Gill was asked to tone them down, and even in 1913 'to remove paint from nipples of "young woman" to please C. K. Butler', a council member of the Society. Gill continued to colour his sculpture, both sacred and secular subjects, throughout his career.

4. The Temple of Love

On the back of both reliefs Gill incised the symbol of a hand with an eye set in its palm. He first carved this device in 1908 as a small wood engraving, at a time when he was getting to know Ananda Coomaraswamy. Gill drew it again against the date of 11 November in his diary for 1910. This was the day after he had had a meeting with Augustus John and Jacob Epstein in London, and Gill had stayed the night with Epstein. Gill and Epstein had become professionally close during the Summer of 1910, sharing as they did a commitment to direct carving in stone, and an interest in sculpture that was not Greek and Roman, for example Egyptian and, most significantly, Indian. In January 1911 Gill wrote to William Rothenstein, who was travelling in India: 'Epstein . . . and I agree with you in your suggestion that the best route to Heaven is via Elephanta, Elura and Ajanta'.[20]

¶ On 10 September 1910 Epstein went to stay with Gill at Ditchling in order to inspect an outdoor site on the Sussex Downs as the possible location for a projected new version of Stonehenge which they had recently conceived together. Their grand scheme for a twentieth-century Stonehenge was never written down but clues remain to reveal that Gill and Epstein planned a vast outdoor temple with upright standing stones, carved by themselves, to fit into a grand scheme celebrating the fertile life force of man.

19. *Art-Nonsense and Other Essays*, London, Cassell & Co & Francis Walterson, 1929, p.38

20. Letter 19, *The Letters of Eric Gill*, ed. Walter Shewring, London, Jonathan Cape, 1947, pp.36–7. These were decorated rock-cut Indian temples, dating from the seventh century AD.

Crucifixion 1910
cat.6

A Roland for an Oliver 1910
cat.4

¶ Four sculptures by Gill, all made during plans for the Stonehenge project, bear the symbol of the eye in the hand, a symbol that occurred in Gill's diary when he was discussing these matters with Epstein. For that reason, it may be possible to see these four sculptures as relating in some way to the temple scheme. The four are *Crucifixion* (cat.6), *A Roland for an Oliver* (cat.4), *Ecstasy* (cat.7) and a small relief of *Cupid* (see below). The subject-matter of these four was religious renunciation symbolised by a nude male figure, pagan sensuality provided by a nude female figure, the act of human copulation with nude male and female figures, and a small nude child symbolising the messenger or catalyst for human love.

Cupid 1910
Present whereabouts
unknown

¶ The art critic C. Lewis Hind gathered material in 1910 for a book entitled *The Post-Impressionists*, published in 1911. One chapter of his book was devoted to Post-Impressionism in sculpture and drew information from both Gill and Epstein about their current work. Epstein had recently carved the stone head of Augustus John's young son Romilly and this crudely carved head sat on top of a stone plinth with the letters 'ROM' carved into it by Gill. Epstein revealed to Lewis Hind that 'Rom . . . is the Eternal Child, one of the flanking figures of a group apotheosing Man and Woman, around a central shrine, that the sculptor destines in his dreams for a great temple'. Epstein did not carve a group apotheosing Man and Woman, but Gill's relief *Ecstasy* fits the description well. *Ecstasy* can be seen as the apotheosis of Gill's views at that time on the canonisation and amalgamation of sacred and profane love.
¶ The sources for the male and female figures in *Ecstasy* have been

identified with Gladys, Gill's sister, and Ernest Laughton, her first husband. However, Gill's depiction of a naked human couple involved in the act of copulation, although relating to people he knew very well, has a much more abstract and universal content. Gill wrote that 'All creative acts have God for their author. The human act of begetting is a type of divine creative power.' The lovers in *Ecstasy* are based on intimate friends (indeed Gill began an incestuous relationship with Gladys around this time), but Gill was soon to transform this subject, via many wood engravings and smaller sculptures, into a metaphor for divine love. Perhaps he was able to view his relationship with his sister in the light of making it an act of homage to God. Gill converted most further renderings of this subject into Christ the Bridegroom and Ecclesia, the Church, or His Bride (*see cats 49, 50 and 51*). Medieval theologians, starting with St Ambrose and St Augustine, had proposed an interesting relationship between the Virgin Mary and Christ; because of her position as the vehicle for the incarnation of our Lord, she was considered to be the Bride of God. Likewise, the Church was defined as the Bride of Christ. St Paul enjoined husbands to love their wives 'as Christ also loved the Church and gave Himself for it'.[21] In the Book of Revelation the Church, symbolised as the New Jerusalem, came down from heaven 'prepared as a bride adorned for her husband'.[22]

¶ Gill's *Ecstasy* was not the only sculpture of his to celebrate physical union; a small relief entitled *Votes for Women* (present whereabouts unknown, but a rubbing of it exists) also shares the same subject-matter. The composition shows a naked female adopting a crouched position on top of a recumbent naked male. The title implies that this woman is a new woman who is able to express her

Votes for Women 1910
Present whereabouts
unknown

21. Letter to the Ephesians, 5, v.25

22. Revelation, 21, v.2

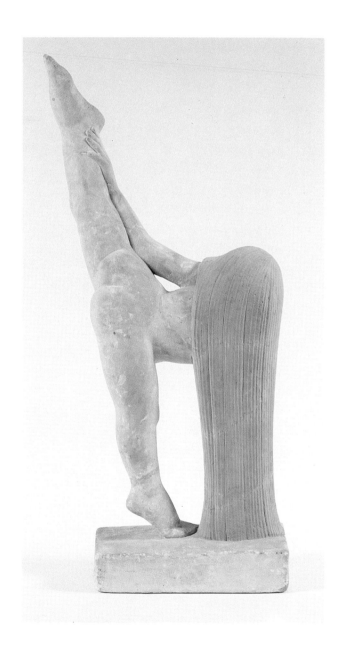

Splits II 1923
cat.56

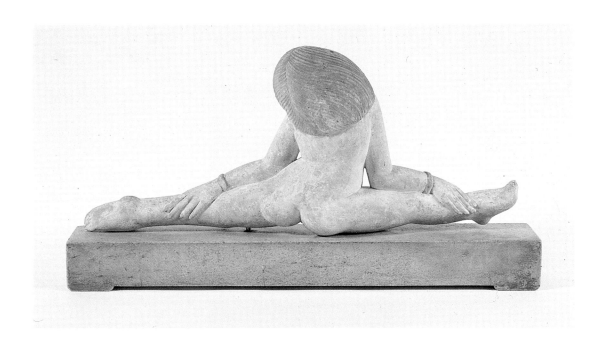

Splits I 1923
cat.54

own will and that her role is a superior one. Both take up quite contorted, even athletic poses which are dictated primarily by the restricting shape of the oval outline which circumscribes the figures.

¶ Figures in athletic poses begin to appear in Gill's sculpture around 1911. A handful of sources suggest their inspiration. The first is a knowledge of Indian temple sculptural programmes such as Elephanta and Elura with their contorted erotic figures; then there is Gill's love of the circus and the music hall. And finally many figures in Western medieval architectural sculpture, especially capitals and misericords, take up acrobatic poses, which are often quite profane in their genital display. Rodin set many of his figures in contorted poses which drew attention to their genital areas. Gill's tumblers and contorted acrobats were usually on a small scale, on average about seven to ten inches in size. They were often conceived with more than one balancing point and therefore could be rotated by hand to take up different orientations, as seen in *The Rower* (*cat.17*). Gill's acrobatic sculptures such as *Splits I* and *Splits II* (*cats 54 and 56*) could be seen as concrete expressions of ideas and emotions and these acrobatic nudes in unashamed revealing poses symbolise complete freedom from inhibition.

The Rower 1912
Standing and seated
cat.17

5. Maillol, Carving and Modelling

At the very beginning of Gill's career as a sculptor, Count Harry Kessler of Weimar attempted to provide him with financial and moral support. Kessler was also a significant patron of the French sculptor Aristide Maillol. Kessler decided that Gill would benefit from a period working as an assistant to Maillol. He obtained Maillol's agreement to the scheme and signed a three-year lease on a house in Marly-le-Roi, a Parisian suburb and Maillol's home, for Gill's use. Gill went along with the scheme to the extent of arriving in Marly-le-Roi but then fled back to Ditchling. He wrote Kessler a letter explaining why he could not work with Maillol. He explained that he had been attracted in the first place because it would afford him the chance to start afresh 'free from the Arts & Crafts Movement – and in the proximity of so splendid a mind as Maillol's'. Maillol could well have appealed to Gill because the French artist, like Gill himself, was self-taught in the field of sculpture; Maillol's art school training had been as a painter. His ideas were his own, thought through in the mind before becoming concrete reality. The benefits of studying with Maillol were thought by Gill to be technical and artistic but on reflection he realised he would learn virtually nothing:

. . . Maillol being more of a modeller than actually a stone carver, technically I should learn nothing . . . I have come to the conclusion that I do not want to learn *pointing* – that I want to be a stone carver – that I do not particularly want to know how to reproduce accurately and expeditiously in stone a clay model. I want to have only so much to do with modelling as is necessary for that kind of client who wants to know what he's going to get before he gets it. And even so I should refuse to guarantee a likeness between the model and the stone. The inspiration comes with the carving and is an entirely different inspiration from that which comes with the clay.[23]

¶ Gill did not publish his views on what sculpture was until 1917, but in this 1910 letter to Kessler, they are set out clearly, probably for the first time. Gill did not want to be a modeller, he wanted to be an artist who cuts things out of stone, figures that allowed the stone partly to dictate their form. From the time of the medieval sculptors until about 1908, most stone sculpture had been made by first modelling the figure in a clay or wax version and then converting this soft, unstable, transitory object into durable stone

23. Letter 13, *The Letters of Eric Gill*, p.28

by means of a pointing machine. This mechanical contraption, with a lot of moveable arms fixed onto a rigid cage, established parallel points on the model and on the stone block about to be carved. Maillol employed stone-carvers to convert his clay models into stone, and it was this step that Gill wished to eschew. Prior to the use of clay or plaster models, which were in vogue from late medieval times until the end of the nineteenth century, earlier sculpture had been created by direct carving, that is by the sculptor carving his figure straight from the block without recourse to a model in a different material. In Britain Gill is credited with bringing the direct carving approach back into use, and his earlier training as a stone-mason and cutter of letters in stone and wood would have given him the technical expertise to reinstate a neglected approach to the making of sculpture. A year earlier, in Paris in 1908, the Romanian sculptor Brancusi had also adopted this method and had carved *The Kiss*, two half-length figures whose forms hardly violate the cubic form of the stone from which they were carved. Other sculptors in Paris also carved directly at this time, notably Derain, Chabaud and Lipchitz. Gill may not have known of these avant-garde statements across the Channel. However he did not need to learn from them because he had numerous examples of direct carving in the London museums he so often frequented, such as Indian and medieval sculpture at the Victoria and Albert Museum and Egyptian and Archaic Greek sculpture at the British Museum.

Clay model
for Gill's figure
for Roger Fry
1910–11

¶ Although Gill derided the method of modelling in clay to create shape, he did make models in clay, plasticine or wax occasionally. There appear to be two reasons for this. Firstly, in order to make a scale model to show to a client, and secondly, so that an edition could be made, for commercial purposes (*see cats 13, 14 and 49*). Also he took plaster casts of parts of human anatomy that he found difficult to carve, so that they could be used for reference purposes; a diary entry for 30 May 1912 records: 'Took cast of Miss Sawyer's foot and Ethel's hand in eve'. In 1910 Roger Fry commissioned a stone figure for his garden at Guildford and Gill spent many hours making a large model in clay. When this had been approved by Fry, Gill paid for a London firm of plaster casters to come to Ditchling and cast the clay model into plaster. He then carved the stone figure by copying the plaster.

¶ This approach cannot have been one that Gill was pleased to employ, but it might indicate a sense of timidity on his part when confronted by a commission for a large stone figure for a prominent place in the garden of an eminent figure in the British art world.

Madonna and Child
plasticine model
1912–13
see
cats 13 and 14

(The figure is now in the Dutch Garden, Holland Park, London.)
If it did indicate caution, that was soon dispelled and it does not
seem that Gill resorted to the use of clay or plaster models again.
If a client needed to see a model before the commission was agreed,
then Gill undertook to provide a set of scale drawings, and a model
in stone, usually one-third of the final size (see *cats 80, 81 and 85*),
or on the scale of one inch to one foot.

¶ In 1912 and 1913 Gill made three small figure groups of the
Madonna and Child from plasticine (see *cats 13, 14 and 16*). He had
plaster editions of twelve made of all of them, and a bronze edition,
probably six, made of two of them. The plaster figures were then
hand-painted by Gill and sold at one pound each, while the bronzes
were priced at £15. They were offered for sale from 1913 at Everard
Meynell's bookshop situated near to Westminster Cathedral,
where they would hopefully be purchased by Catholic worshippers.
An editioned sculpture could be seen in the same light as an
editioned wood engraving; it allowed something well-conceived
and well-made to be appreciated by a wider audience.

6. The Stations of the Cross

¶ Although Gill carved an experimental relief of the *Crucifixion*
(*cat.6*) in 1910, he was called upon to produce the same subject for
others throughout his career as a maker of tombstones. A good
proportion of Gill's figural sculpture is concerned with the figure
of the crucified Christ. He employed small variations but kept
basically to the same style of slim figure with the arms of Christ
positioned at forty-five degrees to the horizontal bar of the Cross.
Only in the 1920s did Gill's figure of Christ become more muscular
and energetic, and less a sacrificial victim (see *cat.44*).

¶ In 1913 Gill carved for himself a small relief of the *Crucifixion*, with
the inscription 'O TE FELICEM' at the bottom of the Cross (*cat. 18*).
This is not a quotation from the Gospels; but in translation reads
'O Happy Thou'. If taken to mean the viewer, then he or she must
be reflecting upon the great gift of God's love for mankind. The
figure of Christ on the Cross, although physically exhausted and at
the point of death, forms his left hand into a gesture of benediction.
Gill uses the same gesture of benediction on three more carved
reliefs of the crucified Christ. These are the Twelfth and
Fourteenth Stations of the Cross in Westminster Cathedral, which
Gill carved during the years 1914–18 (see *cats 32 and 33*) and the
relief shown here.

Crucifixion relief 1913
Present whereabouts
unknown

¶ As Gill found that his conversion to Roman Catholicism was inevitable, he became a frequent visitor to Westminster Cathedral. He and his wife Ethel were received into the Roman Catholic Church on his thirty-first birthday, 22 February 1913, in a church in Brighton. At this very time, the Westminster Cathedral authorities were seeking a suitable artist to make the fourteen Stations of the Cross in relief, in the places left appointed for them on the nave piers by the architect J. F. Bentley. Bentley died in 1902 and John Marshall was appointed cathedral architect in his stead. Gill was introduced to Marshall by a mutual friend as a possible candidate for the making of the Stations:

I was almost unknown in any respectable circles and, I suppose, entirely unknown among catholic ecclesiastics. I believe it is true . . . that had it not been that I was willing to do the job at a price no really 'posh' painter or sculptor would look at, I should certainly never have got it. As it was, the pious donors were getting restive and as the Cardinal Archbishop is said to have said, if the architect didn't hurry up and do something about it, he would give the work to the first catholic he met in the street. So they gave it to me.[24]

¶ Although Gill had only had three years' experience as a sculptor, in 1913 he was given this major commission to produce fourteen large-scale public sculptures for the most prestigious church of the Roman Catholic faith in England. The commission was considered important enough to grant Gill a military dispensation from being called to fight for his country during the First World War.
¶ The iconographic programme of the Stations of the Cross had been codified by the late nineteenth century into fourteen significant episodes during Christ's journey along the Via Dolorosa in Jerusalem, from the time of His condemnation by Pontius Pilate to His burial (see cat.29). As a practising Catholic, Gill knew that the Stations of the Cross were 'furniture' not decorations and that he had to confine himself to 'what might be called a diagrammatic treatment of the subjects'. He equated what he had to do in stone with what in words is called 'plain language' and in music 'plain chant'. As they began to be set onto the nave piers of the cathedral, so the critical coverage grew. Journalists had to search around for adjectives to describe the style in which Gill worked, and two much in use were 'Neo-Byzantine' and 'Assyrian'. Gill replied to the critics:

I gather . . . that it is generally supposed that I am endeavouring to imitate some bygone style. Critics always say that I am a person who attempts to be Egyptian or Syrian, or something or other. That is simply not the case. I am working in the only style in which I can work. I am not a learned antiquarian who can work in any style at choice.[25]

Trial panel for the
Fifth Station of the Cross
1913

¶ It was a little disingenuous of Gill to say he was not a learned anti-quarian because his youthful years at Chichester had been mostly occupied in exploring every nook and cranny of the medieval cathedral there. Equally, as he travelled around the country on inscription and tombstone commissions, he regularly made a point of visiting medieval village churches and wayside crosses, and on a visit to York Cathedral he particularly sought out the twelfth-century stone relief of the Virgin and Child, as he did the West Front of Wells Cathedral when in Somerset. As often as he could Gill visited Chartres Cathedral, which was for him the most perfect stone building in the world. However, he admired not only its west doorways decorated with solemn and splendid carved stone figures which proclaimed their theological message, but also the rhythms and proportions of the cathedral as a whole.

¶ Although he was a great admirer of medieval art, his style, as he said, was indeed the only one in which he could work because it

25. 'Mr Gill's reply to the critics', *Observer*, 17 October 1915, p.16

was dictated by his technical training and prowess. Gill marked out his stone reliefs before carving with outlines that indicated the depth to which each part should be cut, by half an inch, an inch, and so on. Then he cut backwards from the front skin of the stone, removing material layer by layer, by following the outlines drawn on the stone. It was a methodical and logical procedure which produced direct yet rather heraldic images. David Kindersley, an apprentice letter-cutter who joined Gill's workshop in the mid-1930s, recalled how Gill worked with sureness and clarity:

His attention was remarkable in degree and duration . . . No tool was ever forced beyond its capacity. All stages were in process at once over various parts of the carving, the projections always being a stage ahead so that, for all the world, it appeared a simple question of removing a series of skins of differently textured stone. Strength and firmness of form were assured not only by the clarity of his vision but in no small degree through his technique. All form for Mr Gill was of a convex order. Concavities were the result of the meeting of two convexities.[26]

7. Ditchling and T.O.S.D.

In 1907 Gill had moved out of London to the village of Ditchling in Sussex, in order to escape the commercialism of the metropolis. Letter-cutting and tombstones could be carved anywhere and a spacious workshop in a country village was better than cramped conditions in London. Edward Johnston, the scribe, moved there in 1912 and another colleague from London, Hilary Pepler, who had run a working men's club in Hammersmith, joined them in 1915, giving his reason as 'an excuse to follow the prophet into the wilds'. Pepler was a Quaker who converted to Roman Catholicism in 1917 through Gill's influence. Pepler also ran a hand press at Ditchling and this allowed Gill's views to find an immediate if limited voice. ¶ Gill devoted a section of his *Autobiography* to an examination of his life as a member of the Third Order of St Dominic. He was introduced to this path of monastic life in 1918 by his friend Desmond Chute whom he had recently met, and the lay order was instituted at Ditchling, with Gill, Chute and Hilary Pepler as founder members. These Tertiaries of the Order of St Dominic founded the Guild of St Joseph and St Dominic as a guild of Catholic craftsmen. Pepler announced that 'The object . . . is to replace the worship of Mammon by the worship of God'. And in his *Autobiography* Gill did not pass over the opportunity for some proselytising on behalf of the Guild:

26. David Kindersley, 'Mr Gill', in *The Life and Works of Eric Gill*, p.62

Thus it was that we became Tertiaries of the Order of St Dominic. We could not go so far as to say that *all* Christian men and women must . . . engage themselves by vow or promise to live according to one or another of the Religious rules . . . But in the complete mess which the men of business have made of the modern world – for though sinners will make a mess anyway, the particularly beastly and disastrous mess in which we find ourselves today is the product of the particular beastliness of men of business – it does seem as though as many as possible should enrol themselves under the disciplines offered by Religion in the special sense of the Religious Orders.[27]

¶ A major commission came Gill's way during his Ditchling years, which he cunningly used to rebuke the 'beastliness of men of business'. The commission was to carve a large stone relief of 'Christ Driving out the Money Changers from the Temple' as the Leeds University War Memorial (*cat.44*). Sir Michael Sadler, Vice Chancellor of Leeds University, had been impressed by drawings of this subject that Gill had submitted in 1916 for a London County Council competition to design a memorial to honour their staff killed during the First World War (*cats 45 and 46*). Gill's drawings had been admired and awarded a prize but not used, so Sadler gave Gill the chance to make the work for Leeds.

¶ Gill sat to William Rothenstein for a portrait drawing in July 1916, and while forced to keep still, he found he had two alternative paths of thought. One was 'thinking about women (in some detail)' and the other a suitable subject for his London County Council design. 'The former subject of cogitation seemed irresistible and I began on that, but somehow I got shunted on to the other subject and it suddenly occurred to me that the act of Jesus in turning out the buyers and sellers from the Temple as he did was really a most courageous act and most warlike.'[28] Gill was not afraid to take a moral stance against social evils, the root of which he felt was the desire for money, and here was a chance to announce his message in concrete form. He wrote to Geoffrey Keynes in excited terms about the commission:

I'm thinking of making it a pretty straight thing – modern dress as much as poss., Leeds manufacturers, their wives and servants . . . Not that I'm thinking to revert to my first stage – the artist as prophet and preacher – the Chenil Gallery stage – because there's no need. Here is the sermon given into my hands, so to

27. *Autobiography*, p.211

28. Letter 57, *The Letters of Eric Gill*, p.82

say . . . I'm only the aesthetic instrument of the moralists and phil-osophers. But there's no need to apologize . . . Even as artist I may well be enthusiastic quite apart from the fact that, as citizen of this great country and member of Christ's Bride, I rather like . . . the revolutionary job of turning out the money-changers.[29]

The Leeds War Memorial
in progress
1922
see cat.44

¶ Gill carved the large relief between April 1922 and April 1923 and it was unveiled in Leeds by the Bishop of Ripon on 1 June 1923 to strong local criticism about its subject-matter. It depicted Christ with a seven-pronged whip symbolising the seven deadly sins, and the hound of St Dominic at his heels, driving out six figures in modern-day dress. Gill stated that he had clothed these figures in contemporary fashion because the point of the sculpture was 'ethi-cal rather than historical or archaeological'. The men of business from the West Riding of Yorkshire felt that it was they who were being personally attacked, rather than the German economic ambitions which led to the First World War, and for which the sculpture acted as a memorial. Gill was unrepentant; he had chosen the subject 'for it commemorates the most just of all wars – the war of Justice against Cupidity – a war waged by Christ himself'.[30] It was a profoundly stimulating subject for him. When asked by the British Government in 1935 to carve a huge relief for the Headquarters in Geneva of the League of Nations (*cat.100*), Gill again suggested it, but this time was prepared to consider an alternative.

29. Letter 66, *The Letters of Eric Gill*, p.99

30. 'A War Memorial', *Art-Nonsense and Other Essays*, p.110

8. Capel-y-ffin

Gill went to Capel-y-ffin to free himself from the increasing pub-
licity that surrounded his role within the Ditchling community.
Early in 1924 he heard about a ruinous nineteenth-century Welsh
monastery at Capel-y-ffin, in the midst of the Black Mountains,
and fifteen miles from the nearest town of Abergavenny. The
monastery at Capel belonged to a mother community of Benedict-
ine monks on Caldey Island, off the South Wales coast near Tenby,
and the monks were willing to have Gill and his family, and two
other families – the Attwaters and the Cribbs – as tenants. 'Three
families left Ditchling – three fathers, three mothers, seven children . . . one pony, chickens, cats, dogs, goats, ducks and geese, two
magpies and the luggage' and arrived at Capel in a 'steady Welsh
downpour' on 14 August 1924.[31] There were no modern amenities
at Capel, which meant much labour for Gill's wife and three
daughters, who also managed the attendant twenty-acre farm.
¶ Because there was no ideal space for a large stone-carving workshop, Gill's four years at Capel were mainly occupied with lettered
inscriptions, tombstones and wood engraving. These were the
years when Gill was friendly with Robert Gibbings who ran the
Golden Cockerel Press, and also when he first made contact with
Stanley Morison, the typographical adviser to the Monotype Cor-
poration for whom Gill designed the superb typefaces of Perpetua
and Gill Sans.
¶ 'If "Ditchling" may be thought of as the period of my spiritual
schooldays . . . so "Capel-y-ffin" must be thought of as the period
of my spiritual puberty':[32] these were the unusual phrases with
which Gill described the underlying quality of his Welsh period in
his *Autobiography*. The age of puberty in a growing human is the
state of being functionally capable of procreation, and Gill refers
to his Capel years as ones in which he was 'more dispassionately
to review and probe' into questions about human love and sex.
The handful of sculptures produced at Capel, including the
Deposition (*cat.62*) and *The Sleeping Christ* (*cat.67*), could be seen
to have a greater sense of tender, deep sensuality than those
produced at Ditchling. The exception is the large *Crucifixion* of
1925 (*cat.66*), which is almost expressionist in its agonised
intensity.

31. *Autobiography*,
p.216

32. *Autobiography*,
p.223

9. Deo Omnipotenti

Gill left Capel-y-ffin on 11 October 1928 for a quadrangle of decent brick buildings in rural Buckinghamshire, and a direct railway line to London:

The removal from Wales to Pigotts, Speen, Bucks., though not undertaken with any such purpose in view, brought about a return to sculpture. At Capel-y-ffin I hadn't had any but small carving jobs, either because architects and people got the idea that I was too far away, or just because there didn't happen to be work for me to do . . . But no sooner did we get to Pigotts than sculpturing works began pouring in.[33]

¶ The commission that placed Gill most prominently before the public was his work for the BBC, even though he pronounced himself not well pleased with it. The Governors of the BBC decided that they would like some sculpture for their new headquarters at Broadcasting House, Portland Place. They requested a group representing *Prospero and Ariel* (see *cat.85*) for the niche over the main door, a figure of *The Sower* (see *cat.82*) for the entrance hall, and three reliefs with scenes of *Ariel* (see *cats 87, 88, 89 and 90*) to be set above the three side doors of the building. Gill was not in favour of architectural sculpture because the sculptor was only 'called in by the architect to titivate a building which, it is supposed, would otherwise be too dull and plain'.[34] However, the BBC commission did not fall into this category because the main sculpture was given its own space, a curved niche. Gill felt that:

A statue in a niche is not architectural sculpture . . . It is not primarily something that the architect wants for the good of his building; it is primarily something wanted by the owner or occupier of the building . . . It does not grow from the architectural necessities, but from the necessities of the building's use. It proclaims who the building belongs to and what game they think they are playing at. The Governors of the BBC imagine they are playing a very high game indeed. Deo Omnipotenti are the first words they hurl at you in their entrance hall, and so the choice of what should be placed in the niche over the main door was obviously a difficult matter.[35]

¶ The Governors appear to have chosen the subject of Prospero and

33. *Autobiography*, p.248

34. 'Prospero and Ariel', *The Listener*, 15 March 1933, p.397

35. Ibid

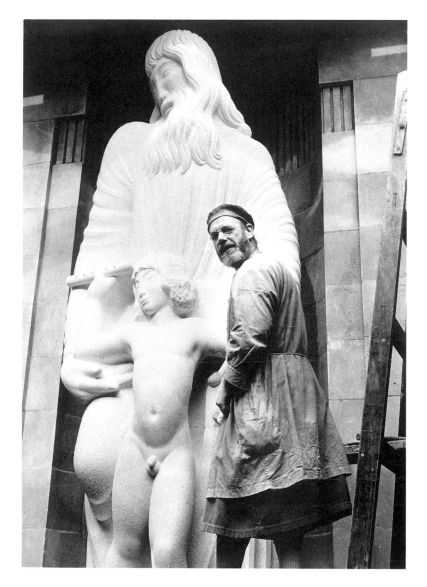

Gill with *Prospero and Ariel*
1932
see cat.85

Ariel from Shakespeare's play *The Tempest* because Ariel was an
'airy spirit', a superficial reference to the airwaves of broadcasting,
who carried out the wishes of Prospero, Duke of Milan, presumably
the Governors. Although they asked for secular characters, Gill
decided to alter their terms of reference:

Had not Prospero power over the immortal Gods? At any rate it
seemed to be only right and proper that I should see the matter
in as bright a light as possible and so I took it upon me to portray
God the Father and God the Son. For even if that were not
Shakespeare's meaning it ought to be the BBC's.[36]

¶ In the half-size model that Gill carved of the *Prospero and Ariel*

36. *Autobiography*,
p.249

group, he cut stigmata into Ariel's upraised hands. They are also there in the full-size group above the main door. The purpose of doing this was to transform Ariel into Christ. For Gill, Ariel was a spirit who assumed flesh and blood and therefore was a significant example of an incarnation. Ariel is shown with his arms raised as if in the act of supplication and this mirrors Christ's sacrifice upon the Cross.

¶ In 1933 Gill converted another secular commission into a sacred one, this time for the Directors of the London, Midland and Scottish Railway. He carved for them a large relief of Odysseus being greeted by Nausicaa (cat.93), a subject taken from Homer's Odyssey and one that was meant to symbolise hospitality. This relief was the dominant feature of the dining room of the Midland Hotel, Morecambe, and although the subject-matter was unusual, it had a lively pagan quality. However, Gill described the relief as 'a holy picture' in a letter to his friend G. K. Chesterton, adding that 'the LMS don't know that'. Although Gill does not explain what he meant by 'a holy picture', the relief seems to symbolise the Christian view of loving service as taught in Christ's last eschatological discourses before the sequence of events that led inexorably to His death, epitomised in the following phrases found in the Gospel according to St Matthew, 25, vv.35–6: 'For I was hungry and you gave me food; I was thirsty and you gave me drink; I was a stranger and you made me welcome; naked and you clothed me'. The four short phrases from Matthew correspond closely to the actions and attributes of the four women who wait upon Odysseus. One offers food, another drink, Nausicaa stretches out her hand in welcome and the fourth provides a length of cloth.

¶ The main thread of Gill's life and work was basically an unceasing examination of the question that Job had dared to ask – 'What is man?', and having confronted that, then to ask 'What is man's purpose on earth?'. He was acutely aware that

It is a comparatively simple matter to shape a stone to one's liking, but the devils themselves conspire to hinder man's efforts to shape his own life. Therefore, though not every man is called to the life of 'religion', every man is called to the love of God and every man is called to give love to the work of his hands.[37]

Although Gill was fond of describing man as both matter and spirit, he was always prepared to acknowledge that the pre-eminent partner in that duality was the spirit. His Autobiography, written at

37. 'Art and Love', in Art-Nonsense and Other Essays, p.198

speed and with great honesty and integrity in the last months of his life, was less a historical narrative with detailed facts than a history of the growth and development of the spirit and soul of an artist. He was proud of the fact that he was self- taught as a sculptor; art schools bred a conventional response to things and stressed the naturalistic. Gill wanted to make things that were clear, rational, imaginative and hieratic. He created a mental, spiritual and formal environment that was unique in twentieth-century British art and one which has no real successors. In a letter to Desmond Chute, he gives an inkling of his fundamental beliefs:

You cannot certainly paint a good picture by going to an art school and learning a method, but must fall in love with God first and last – that is not art you can be taught but only technical things (eg. to keep your hand & brushes clean and your lines clear . . .) – so you cannot certainly walk with God by following a method, but must wait upon Him as a lover – singing beneath his window – waiting for him in the snow.[38]

38. Letter 107, *The Letters of Eric Gill*, p.154

'Sculpture:
An Essay by Eric Gill',
first published in
The Highway, June 1917,
reprinted by Douglas Pepler,
Ditchling, Sussex, 1918

Sculpture

I shall assume that the word sculpture is the name given to that craft and art by which things are cut out of a solid material, whether in relief or in the round. I shall not use the word as applying to the craft and art of modelling. I oppose the word 'cut' to the word 'model' and assume that a sculptor is one who shapes his material by cutting and not by pressing. The cutting of stone is the type of the craft of the sculptor and the modelling of clay, if he practises it at all, is, for him, merely a means of making preliminary sketches. The modelling of clay or wax whether the thing modelled is to be rendered permanent by firing in an oven or by casting in metal or plaster, is a craft and art of the greatest importance, but facility in it is no sort of necessity for the carver.

¶ By the word 'thing' I mean that which is its own justification, as opposed to (1) that of which the justification is the success with which it imitates the appearance of something else and (2) that of which the justification is the success with which it conveys a criticism or appreciation – e.g. the work of Cimabue as opposed to (1) that of a photographer and (2) that of Rembrandt.

¶ A work of art may resemble another thing or it may not, but such resemblance as it may have must be thought of as accidental and not substantive.

¶ Representations can and may, undoubtedly, be made by cutting and modelling, but such is not primarily the sculptor's job. The sculptor's job is primarily that of making *things*, not representations or criticisms of things.

¶ It is commonly supposed that the study of nature is a prime necessity and that realism, which is thought to be the close imitation of appearances, is the object of the artist. Now in the first place the study of nature is *not* a prime necessity, though the love of nature may be such, and in the second place realism is not the imitation of appearances but is an expression of the reality underlying appearances.

¶ That kind of sculpture which is dependent upon a close study and imitation of appearance is only very little removed from the craft of the photographer – an admirable craft but not primarily the sculptor's.

¶ The sculptor, as any other artist, is primarily a herald, and his work heraldic. His business is to achieve in the things he makes the discovery of Beauty and to proclaim it. By the word 'Beauty' I do not mean merely the loveliness of the earth or of living things, but that absolute entity which, like Goodness and Truth is apprehended by conscience.*

¶ The analysis of this matter is the business of the aesthetician, to whom the artist would do well to leave it. Let the artist mind his own business, remembering that the study of heraldry is the study proper to him as artist – that is the study, not merely of coats of arms, but of all those means by which Beauty has been and may be discovered or revealed – and that nature is for him simply a dictionary, however well-beloved and however inspiring, to which he may go for reference when necessary or when he chooses.

¶ Now there are two ways of regarding works of art. Such works may be thought of as having existed only incompletely in the mind or imagination of the artist and as having awaited completion in, and as having been dependent upon the material of which they are made, so that the artist and the material are jointly and not severally responsible for the finished work, or such works may be thought of as having existed completely in the mind of the artist and as having a merely accidental relation to such stuff as he has chosen for their material embodiment.

¶ Thus we may say that there are two kinds of works of art: first, those which owe part of their quality as works of art to the material of which they are made and of which the material inspires the artist and is freely accepted by him, and, second, those which owe nothing of their quality except by accident, to their material and, indeed, of which the material is even a hindrance to the free expression of the artist and is patronised rather than beloved by him.

¶ Of the first kind are all primitive works and the works of barbarians. Of this kind, also, are the works of all those craftsmen and artists who are not merely designers and who are accustomed to translate their own ideas or designs into the natural terms of material and are free to do so.

¶ Of the second kind are the works of artists and designers who are only executants in the material of which the

* See Note on Beauty, p. 50.

Seated Mother and Child (detail) 1913

design or model and not the finished work is made. Thus all works designed in clay by the artist and translated into stone by an artisan are of this kind.

¶ Now I do not suppose myself to be addressing those who are engaged in designing things for other people to make or those who are engaged in the job of modelling clay for casting in bronze or firing in kilns. I am addressing the ordinary workman who, like myself, has in hand the job of carving stone.

¶ There are two chief kinds of stone-carving. Just as a tailor may cut his coat according to his cloth or his cloth according to his coat, so a stone carver may make his carving according to his stone or he may cut his stone according to the preconception of his carving which is in his mind or which is necessitated by the building or other place where his carving is to go.

¶ Thus if you have a piece of stone you may, if you are free to do so carve it into what shape you will; but if your carving is to fit a certain place, either in size or manner, you will have to be very sure before you begin to work, as to your measurements and as to your subject and its treatment. Therefore the two kinds of stone-carving may be called the 'unconditioned' and the 'conditioned'. Now for either of these two kinds it may be useful or necessary to make a model, but if such be made it should be made in soft stone and to some simple scale, such as 'one inch to the foot' or 'quarter full size', so that measurements may be easily calculated from it. It is not desirable to make it to the full size because a full-size model is not worth the labour unless the proposed carving is to be no more than a few inches high, and then a model is generally unnecessary and often undesirable.

¶ It is not desirable to make the model in clay, because the sort of thing which can be easily and suitably constructed in clay may not be, and generally is not, suitable for carving in stone.

¶ The armature, that is the skeleton of iron or wood which is necessary for the support of the clay for a model of a large size, is not merely difficult to make, but has the effect of giving a quite different character to the work from that which is the natural character of carved stone. The armature, in fact, is the model – the model reduced to its simplest terms of movement and attitude.

¶ Modelling in clay is properly not (except for such very small things as can be held and turned about in the hand) the mere pressing and squeezing of the clay into a desired or approved shape. It is rather the clothing or giving of body to a skeleton. It is a process of addition; whereas carving is a process of subtraction.

¶ The proper modelling of clay results, and should so result, in a certain spareness and tenseness of form and any desired amount of 'freedom' or detachment of parts. The proper carving of stone, upon the other hand, results, and should so result, in a certain roundness and solidity of form with no detachment of parts. Consequently a model made to the full size of the proposed carving would be, if modelled in a manner natural to clay, more of a hindrance than a help to the carver, and would be labour, and long labour, in vain.

¶ Further, it must be remembered that enthusiasm is not cheap and lightly to be expended. If a man has really devoted himself to the making of a full-size model of clay or any other material, it is hardly possible for him to face the copying of his own model in stone. He cannot do the same thing twice with the same feeling of propulsion. For that reason, if for no other, it is usual for the work of translation into stone from a full-size model of clay or plaster to be given over to an artisan who proceeds by measurements and various mechanical contrivances to produce an imitation in stone of a thing of which the nature is clay.* The modeller then reappears and gives the finishing touches. The finished work is not a piece of carving, but a stone imitation of a clay model. If the model be good it is possible that the stone imitation may retain some of its goodness.

¶ But why, indeed, should a process so elaborate and so unnatural be followed? It cannot be only because the making of a full-size model has used up the energy of the artist. That might happen once. But an artist who found his energy thus 'used up' would say: 'No, a full-size model is too much of a good thing. I will make only a small model, or none at all, and save myself for the stone.' Why, then, is this process pointing not exceptional nowadays but usual? The answer is simple. It is because artists are not trained in workshops to be stone-carvers, but in art schools to be modellers. There is just this excuse for them: stone-carving is not only very like hard work, especially in its preliminary stages, but it is apparently much slower. If the artist has an idea, that idea is much more quickly materialised in clay than in stone. It is not exactly that he is in a hurry, it is rather that he is feverish, that he is impatient, that he is afraid of losing the

* This work of translation is called 'pointing', and the artisan a 'pointer', because the instrument chiefly used is called a 'pointing machine'. This instrument is one by the aid of which innumerable holes of various depths are drilled in the stone block so that eventually nothing remains to be done but knock off the stone between the holes.

idea in the slow process of stone-cutting.

¶ The later stages of the making of a model in clay are, I think, considerably more irksome and 'nervous', and certainly slower, than the later stages of stone-carving. But in the early stages clay is certainly the easier and more expeditious material.

¶ So it is that clay modelling is so much in vogue: because in the preliminary stages it produces quick results and because clay is the material in which the artist is as a student taught to work.*

¶ Now we have divided works of art into two kinds: those owing their nature in part to their material and those of which the material is accidental. And we have divided stone-carvings into two classes: the unconditioned and the conditioned. It is obvious that if you are an idealist and do not care in what material your idea takes shape, you might just as well or better, be a modeller as anything else. It therefore follows that if I am, as I say, addressing stone-carvers I am not addressing idealists. I am addressing that kind of artist who finds in his material a complement to himself, and that material being stone, it follows that modelling in clay must for him be kept in a wholly subordinate position and be the means, merely, of making such preliminary and experimental sketches as cannot be done on paper.

¶ But the making of models is not absolutely essential. Some stone-carvers may find a model desirable, some may not, or a model may be desirable in one case and not in another. There is, however, little doubt that the use of models is very much overdone at the present time. In the case of carvings in low relief, for instance, a model is generally unnecessary, a drawing to scale being all that is required, and even that may sometimes be dispensed with.

¶ The cause of this over-reliance on models is, as I have said, simple enough: The artist is not trained to be a stone-carver, the stone-carver is not, or is not thought to be, an artist. The artist therefore, becomes a mere designer, the stone-carver a mere executant – the one losing himself in idealism, the other in technical dexterity.

* I think all that is vital in modelling can be written in one paragraph. The model should be seen as a number of contours joined by planes. The best modelling is done by pressing with a tool, and not by squeezing with the fingers. Modelling is the addition of clay to clay, each additional piece of clay being pressed into place with the tool. The use of the fingers is to be avoided as being too facile and as productive of accidental contours and planes. The workman may take advantage of accidents, but this method should not be provocative of such. Hardness and firmness both of intention and execution should be the aim of the modeller as of all workmen, but more particularly of the modeller because of the pliability of his material and the ease with which it may seduce him.

¶ Truly it would be better were 'artist' and 'craftsman' interchangeable terms. But such a consummation is, except in the case of individuals, not possible under modern conditions. The very nature of modern civilisation is such as to preclude it.

¶ Our modern civilisation, admirable as it may appear to be in many of its manifestations of power and goodwill, is, essentially, built upon the employment of the many by the few. It is a complicated system in which world-markets have taken the place of local markets, and factories the place of small workshops, the manufacturer that of the craftsman, the contractor that of the builder, and in which commerce is paramount and men of commerce our rulers.

¶ Altogether apart from the question as to whether it is good or bad is the fact that the combination of craftsman and artist in one individual is foreign to such a civilisation and impossible in it. It is impossible because in such a civilisation men are not commonly their own masters any more than they are commonly their own landlords.

¶ But the question of 'good or bad' cannot be escaped, and our answer to it must be such as is natural to our own point of view as stone-carvers. We cannot make decisions for others. We can, and must, decide for ourselves.

¶ If we are going to be stone-carvers, then we must be both craftsmen and artists. If that combination is impossible, then stone-carving is, as an occupation worthy of free men, non-existent and we must find another trade.

¶ Now I am not looking at this matter from the point of view of the 'artist'. From his point of view there is little of which to complain – he is what he chooses to be. I am looking at the matter from the point of view of the workman, the hired stone-carver. Reform must come at his demand. He is the victim, his must be the revolution.

¶ Men do not eat because other people kindly give them bread. They eat because they are hungry and they would bake bread whether other people were benevolent or not. Even so material organisation and betterment must be the product of appetite and not of theory, of the men and not of their masters, of the players and not of the spectators.

¶ The modern movements of reform fail for this very reason: that they make their appeal to irresponsible persons, to manufacturers and distributors, to shopkeepers and their customers, to anyone but the person responsible for the doing of the work.

¶ Therefore, as men have revolted and have organised with the object of gaining economic independence, so must they revolt and organise to obtain intellectual independence. The trade union must be not merely the guardian of the just price, it must become, as it did the medieval fraternities, the guardian of good quality. The control of industry is valueless unless it includes the control of design and workmanship.

¶ But where all are agreed that the price of labour must be 'fair', very few workmen are concerned to assume or demand responsibility for the work done. It cannot be said that there is, at the present time, any widespread and articulate demand upon the part of stone-carvers that they shall be the executants of their own ideas. They are, as a rule, perfectly willing to execute any design that is put before them. They have ceased to think of themselves as artists, or, rather, for they never did so think of themselves, as free men, they accept without demur the tyranny of the architect and modeller. They either do not profess to have any ideas of their own at all, or such ideas as they have are merely those of copyists and imitators of bygone 'styles', and technical accomplishment is their only criterion of excellence.

¶ In the absence then of any articulate demand for freedom and responsibility there is nothing to be done but to create such a demand. The individual must be converted that the mass may be leavened. And in the forefront of our propaganda must be proclaimed the fact that we, the workmen, the men who do the work, are the persons responsible and not the architect and designer, not the contractor, the shopkeeper or the customer.

¶ We will not talk about art. We will demand responsibility, saying that, as we do the work, we will do it as we choose.* The designer can go. The contractor can go. We will sell things at our own workshops and deal directly with our own customers. We shall demand protection from the importation of cheaper and inferior foreign work and we shall abolish the factory and contracting system.

¶ But meanwhile, before these demands, natural to the craftsman but at present inarticulate, can be enforced, what is to be said of existing efforts at reform from above, that is reforms made at the instance of educational theorists, artists, architects and cultured contractors? For the most part nothing need be said, being reforms from above they may be neglected by the persons below. Coming from above they naturally subserve the interests of the employer and buyer rather than those of the craftsman.

¶ Art cannot be taught, and it is best not talked about. It must be spontaneous. It cannot be imposed. But its enemies can be destroyed. Its enemies are irreligion and the offspring of irreligion – commercialism and the rule of the trader. The trader should be subordinate – he has become the head of the State. *Vade Satanas, Laus Deo.*

¶ I say Art cannot be taught. Art education is therefore impossible. The art school is no good to anyone except as a springboard for revolutionists. Learning about art, reading about it, museums and exhibitions, all alike are of no value to the workman. They are the occupation and invention of well-meaning theorists and of dealers. Technical institutes are a different matter. They are both valuable and dangerous. They are valuable inasmuch as they supplement workshop training though they cannot supplant it. They are a danger inasmuch as they tend to make us content with the present inadequacy of the workshop. They supply a superior workman to our employers without doing anything to hinder the development of a system which destroys workmanship. They give our employers a better quality workman without making any demands upon them which jeopardise the system.

¶ But though technical institutes cannot supplant the workshop, they can and do supplant apprenticeship. The general decay of apprenticeship, due solely to the introduction of the factory system and quantitative as opposed to qualitative production, is more to be deplored than almost every other thing which labour has suffered, and its revival should be one of the first endeavours of revolutionists. No system of state-aided or benevolent technical training in schools can take its place.

¶ The matter must here be left at this bald statement of essentials, without its proper support of argument and reference. Sculpture is both a craft and an art. The combination of craft with art must be revived. The revolution must come at the instance of the craftsman and not of the artist. The need is religion and the subordination of the trader. Again: *Laus Deo: vade Satanas!*

---

*Though we claim the right of choice, yet, the reader will note, we admit responsibility. The responsibilities of the workman to his customer and to the community are even more obvious and natural than those of the trader – the trader being out merely to sell things, the workman to make them. Men do not naturally make things which please only themselves. But a shopkeeper will sell anything, whatever he thinks of it. *He is irresponsible.*

NOTE ON BEAUTY (see p. 47)

Beauty is not to be confused with loveliness. Beauty is Absolute, loveliness Relative. The lovely is that which is or represents the lovable. The lovely is lovable relatively to our love of it. Beauty is Absolute and independent of our love. God is Beautiful whether we love Him or do not, but the taste of an apple is lovely only if we taste it and love the taste. The Madonna of Cimabue is beautiful with an Absolute Beauty. The Madonna Sassoferato is lovely because it portrays that kind of woman who is lovable to those who love that kind of woman and in that kind of attitude which is charming to those who are charmed by it.

Madonna and Child 1912
cat.11

Ecstasy 1910-11
cat.7

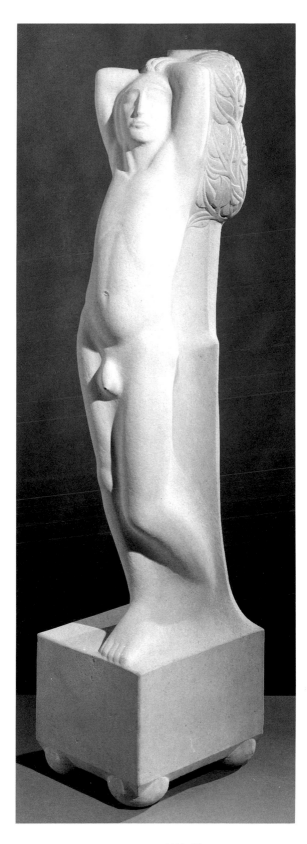

St Sebastian 1919-20
cat.38

Divine Lovers 1922
cat.49

Small Female Torso 1924
cat.61

The Sleeping Christ 1925
cat.67

Tobias and Sara 1926
cat.71

ABSENTES ~ ADSUNT

Left:
Crucifix 1921
cat.48

Rossall School War Memorial Altarpiece 1927
cat.68

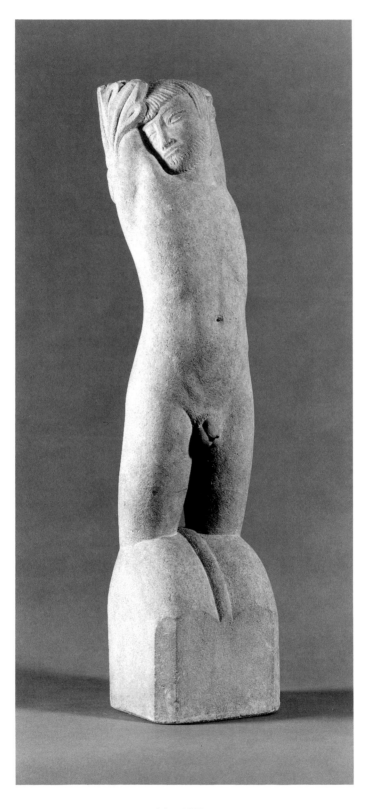

Adam 1927 - 8
cat.78

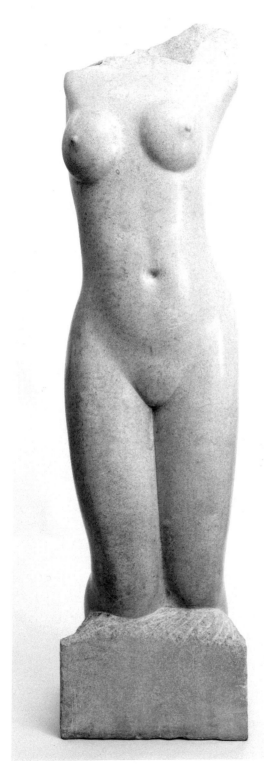

Mankind 1927 - 8
cat.76

Deposition 1924
cat.62

Crucifixion 1925
cat.66

Model for Sculpture:
Prospero and Ariel 1931
cat.85

From Eric Gill,
Art-Nonsense and Other Essays,
London, Cassell & Co
& Francis Walterson, 1929

The Future of Sculpture

The art of sculpture is the making of things in three dimensions such that being seen they please the eye and the mind.

¶ The special department of this art with which we are here concerned is that called FIGURE SCULPTURE.

¶ Figure sculpture is, of course, the making of images of things seen and known, but the degree of likeness to the thing seen or known depends upon innumerable considerations, and varies from what is called 'a speaking likeness' to a simple abstraction. Moreover the thing made may seem to have departed altogether from the sphere of the seen and known and to have entered into that of pure invention or creation.

¶ These three things determine all works of sculpture.

¶ From the point of view of the buyer the 'speaking likeness' is the chief consideration. The artist, the sculptor, though he may, and generally does, to some extent share the point of view of the buyer – the sculptor oscillates between the effort to abstract and the effort to create or invent.

¶ The artist purely as such is the creator; he collaborates with God in creating.

¶ Art improves on Nature. That is what it is for.

¶ Man is artist, man is normally the artist – the maker of things. Man naturally desires good and therefore good things. Man as artist naturally desires to *make* good things – things good in themselves – like God, he would survey his handiwork and see that it is good.

¶ In a broad view of this Universe, man's place is that of God's instrument for a further degree of poignancy in the manifestation of love – of God's love of himself.

¶ So much for man's place as an inhabitant of a material planet. But a creature thus constituted, having free will and consequent responsibility, is necessarily immortal. He is concerned therefore not only with the good of the work (though that be the glory of God and a sufficiently noble concern) but with his own good – his last end. Finis operis, the end of the work, is the business of ART; finis operantis, the end of the worker, is the business of PRUDENCE.

¶ Between these two horns lies the dilemma; for man allowed himself to forget his last end and has consequently inherited a corrupted will and a world full of evil.

¶ Nevertheless, in spite of all the disgusting mess which ill will has brought into existence, man still yearns for his normal occupation as collaborator with God in creating and still endeavours to play the artist. As artist, he starts with the idea of man as right and the world right. On the other hand, the man of prudence, specially so called, the moralist, the ethical teacher, starts with the idea of man as wrong and the world wrong. Both ideas are to be commended, but the man of prudence, the moralist, is, in fact, the more correct. Nevertheless, the artist's forlorn hope is always to be followed, and he will always follow it. He will always be somewhat of a PELAGIAN in practice and will act as though man has never 'fallen' – as though all men were innocent (himself included, which is absurd) and all work were play. And, on the other hand, the moralist will always be something of a PURITAN in practice and will tend to act as though all material activity were essentially evil and art in particular were a devil who, unless chained up to verisimilitude or didacticism, were not to be allowed out.

¶ But all things are mixed – art and prudence inextricably. Even we artists are not entirely devoid of a moral sense, and even moralists have from time to time allowed themselves to be disinterested – for that is the important distinction. For the moralist there is always the question: what will be the result? – to what end is it the means? But for the artist (that normal fellow) the result does not matter; he is not concerned with means, but with things which are ends in themselves.

¶ Hence the besetting sin of the artist is idolatry; an idol is an end that is not God. But the besetting sin of the moralist is money; for money is nothing but a means to something else.

¶ All the best art is religious. Religious means according to the rule of God. All art that is godly, that is, made without concern for worldly advantage, is religious. The great religions of the world have always resulted in great artistic creation because they have helped to set man free from himself – have provided a discipline under which men can work and in which commerce is subordinated.

¶ Inasmuch as the christian artist is employed to represent christian verities, then, as regards what we may call literary content, christian art may be said to be better than non-christian. But literary content is not the primary business of the artist – it is simply something he is employed for and paid to do. A good artist will do it well – a bad artist will do it badly. A good artist is not simply an artist with a good subject. A good artist is simply a man who apprehends and submits to the will of God for the work – as a good man is one who apprehends and submits to the will of God for the deed.

It is by now quite clear that the future of sculpture is the Museum. I mean, of course, the immediate future. Ultimately, or in the far distant future, man will undoubtedly return to a new beginning. The present state of things cannot last for ever; it is founded upon an unnatural condition. In the nature of things man is a responsible creature; he has free will. What he does, what he makes, are things for which he is responsible. The present organisation of industry deprives all but a few artists of any responsibility whatever. The bulk of things made to-day are made under what we call factory conditions, and those conditions are such that of no factory article can you say any man was responsible for making it – it is simply the result of a number of men doing precisely what they were told to do. It is true that the majority of factory hands are content with this condition and even seek to make it absolute. The servile state, however we may jib at the sound of the words, is not only a thing in being – it lacks only legal sanction – it is a thing which most workmen of to-day desire and demand. The appetite for freedom and responsibility is no longer urgent. All that is demanded is security of employment and adequate remuneration and amusement. Nevertheless, this is an unnatural condition, though it is the natural result of industrialism, and while we continue to conduct our affairs on industrial lines, with men of commerce as our rulers and commercial success as our one criterion, we can look for nothing else. Let those who like it enjoy it while it lasts. After all it has its advantages. Innumerable conveniences of daily life are obtainable to-day which were hitherto beyond the dreams of avarice. Queen Elizabeth could not use a telephone. King Alfred had no fountain pen. Orpheus never 'listened in'.
¶ But the reduction of the majority of men and women (for women also are – and with avidity – embracing industrial life) to a sub-human condition of irresponsibility as regards the product of their labour is essentially against nature and therefore against God. Never mind – that is not here my affair. I am not concerned with that. I am concerned with the 'future of sculpture' and must confine my attention to the immediate future.
¶ Sculpture is, in the special sense of figure sculpture and decorative carving, the making of abstractions, inventions and representations in three dimensions. Now, such things cost money: that is to say, they occupy time which might otherwise be used for supplying the immediate needs of the body – food and shelter. If men are going to spend their time in such an occupation someone has got to feed and house them. That's clear. That has always been clear. Who is going to do it? On the answer to this question the future depends. Who is the customer of the artist? Who provides him with bread and butter? And, as regards my special subject, who is going to provide bread and butter for sculptors?
¶ It is clear enough that in the past the bulk of the employment of sculptors was in connection with architecture and it is also clear that the bulk of architectural sculpture was ecclesiastical. That is understandable enough. Religion and churches offer a natural field for such things. I am not now concerned with the reasons for this, and any way it is not a difficult matter. What I am concerned with is the fact that the Church is no longer the 'best buyer' of art in general or of sculpture in particular. The Church is no longer of paramount importance in human affairs. Underneath the surface she still wields the most important influence, and in that distant future with which I am not concerned, she will emerge again into the front line of governors. But at present and in the immediate future we may count the Church as being down and out as far as we are concerned. The Church has always bought freely and without discrimination what was nearest to hand – she has always bought in the cheapest market, and when the ideas, the fundamental ideas, governing the market were ideas for the propagation and support of which she was directly responsible (because she was the chief voice in matters of the mind), in such a time there was nothing to complain of – church work corresponded with Church teaching. But to-day the country is no longer governed by Church teaching – far from it. The result is that church art and Church teaching have nothing in common, and artists can no longer look to her for employment except as an exceptional stroke of luck. The Church, I mean of course the Catholic Church, is not a cultured set – she knows nothing of art – she buys what is to hand. It is not her fault if what is to hand is not worth buying. She is concerned with the end of MAN – hence her pre-occupation with faith and morals, in which alone is she inerrant. And the practical application of faith and morals is prudence. The Church

is not concerned with the end of man's WORK – hence she is not an authority on aesthetics and knows nothing of art.
¶ To-day it is clear that our real governors are the men of commerce, and they also, like the Church before them, buy in the cheapest market, and to-day the ideas of the market are the ideas of men of commerce undiluted by any 'other worldly' considerations whatever – the nearest approach to other-worldliness being contained in such phrases as 'safety first', 'honesty is the best policy', and 'enlightened self-interest'. The market for works of art – works of sculpture – is therefore governed by persons of even less cultural pretensions than were possessed by ecclesiastical governors and the makers of such things can look to men of commerce with even less confidence. If ecclesiastics naturally delight in large and grand churches, men of commerce naturally delight in large and grand banks and insurance buildings. True, they will seek to have these covered with sculptures, and will order corinthian capitals by the dozen and many elegant ladies reclining over doorways, but such things are themselves merely the production of commercial enterprise and are supplied by the contractor on the same principles as the drains – and this is as it should be. Such things are not sculpture in the special sense in which I and we are interested. The special kind of sculpture with which I am concerned is that which is the product of MEN, not mere contractor's hacks; of ARTISTS, not mere factory hands. For such work there is no place on modern building. How could there be? The best modern architects are now quickly coming to see this. There is a laudable tendency among architects to eschew all sculpture and to confine themselves to plain building. Sad as this may be from the point of view of sculptors (for architecture must always offer the best opportunity for sculpture and the collaboration of architect and sculptor must always be the dream of both), sad as the present tendency must be, nevertheless it would be sadder still to continue the worn-out pretence. There is, in fact, no compatibility between the work of a man who does not merely care for his work but for whom his work is the most important thing in life – the one thing worth doing – and that of the gang of more or less unwilling slaves, the more or less doped employees of a modern building contractor. The modern architect is right – let the sculpture go. Let him confine himself to the scale and proportion of his building. Sculpture is unnecessary. From the pyramid of Cheops to the unfinished interior of Westminster Cathedral, architectural grandeur has never been dependent on sculpture.

¶ This essentially optimistic view of the matter – for it is optimistic thus to take it for granted that reasonableness will so far prevail in the immediate future – this optimistic view leads us to the statement with which I began – the future for sculpture is the Museum. There is, of course, the mantelshelf. But what is the mantelshelf but everyman's own little home museum? And what are private collectors but the owners of private museums? I make no complaint of this state of things. 'It's no good', as you may have heard, 'crying over spilt milk', and the milk of human kindness to art and artists is completely spilt and the pitcher broken into a million fragments. And, as also you may have heard, 'we can't be ancient Britons' or 'put back the clock'. These home truths are very salutary. We've jolly well got to take things as they are – we artists. The time is past when it seemed worth while to band ourselves into 'Arts and Crafts Movements' and to join 'Fabian Societies', or 'Art Workers' Guilds'. The business of 'social reform' is outside the sphere of artists. Their business is to get on with the work and leave government and social reform to men of prudence.
¶ Get on with the work. And let no sculptor complain that there is no work or that he has no work to do. There is always stone or clay lying about, and if it should happen that he can find no one to buy his work, then it is simply up to him to consider whether some branch of commercial enterprise is not perhaps his true vocation. It may well be so.
¶ And one very important result of thus setting the sculptor free from any collaboration with the Church or commerce or architecture is that he is thus enabled to try innumerable amusing experiments in purely aesthetic development. He need no longer be didactic or expository or anecdotal to please sentimental ecclesiastics. Nor need he be merely imitative or naturalistic or clever and intricate to please princes of commerce, whose one idea is aggrandisement. Nor need he work in this style or that to satisfy the requirements of some architect or suffer the pain of seeing his works of love stuck in contact with machine-made masonry. He is free from all such things.
¶ But, swept and garnished, he is beset by seven other devils. Now the warfare is purely spiritual. What is beauty? What is 'significant form'? What is the connection between the idea in the mind and the material under the hand? How much is the one dependent on the other? So we return to our beginnings, and like a cave man carving a bone we can again find in art the pure delight of the intelligence collaborating with God in creating.

The Catalogue

The sculptures proceed in a chronological sequence, while related two-dimensional materials – drawings, prints, rubbings – are grouped around particular three-dimensional works, and have their own chronological sequence in relation to the sculpture. The wood engravings are given their P number from John Physick's Victoria and Albert Museum catalogue of Gill's engraved work (published 1963). Measurements of works are given in inches followed by centimetres, with height preceding width and depth. The exhibitions at which the works were first shown are listed, where known. All exhibitions are London venues unless otherwise stated.

League of Nations 'Creation' Relief (detail)
1935
see cat.100

1 Design for Sculpture: Estin Thalassa

1909
Pencil, $17\frac{1}{2} \times 22$ in / 43.7×56 cm
Inscr: *These are the drawings / for the first figure / carving*
EG ever did (Ditchling / 1910) / The actual stone / was bought by /
Count Kessler
Art Collection, Harry Ransom Humanities
Research Center, The University of Texas
at Austin (935)

This is one of four preparatory drawings that Gill made before
carving his first figure sculpture at the end of 1909. (Gill's date
of 1910 on the drawing was added at a later date and is in-
accurate.) The sculpture, of a naked female supporting a tablet
lettered with a Greek inscription, was carved exactly as shown
in this drawing. However, the drawing is probably larger than
the actual stone, whose whereabouts are unknown (see p.19).
The Greek inscription beginning 'Estin Thalassa [There is the
sea]' is taken from Aeschylus' play *Agamemnon*. The sculpture
was the first that Gill ever exhibited in an exhibition. He sent
it to the Whitechapel Art Gallery's mixed Spring exhibition in
May 1910, where he described it as 'Tablet for the wall of a
seaside house' and priced it at £40. He sold it to Count Harry
Kessler of Weimar for £20 in April 1912.

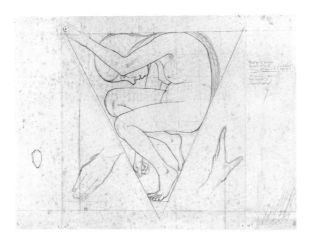

2 Mother and Child

1910
Portland stone, $24\frac{1}{2} \times 8 \times 6\frac{3}{4}$ in / $62.2 \times 20.3 \times 17.1$ cm
Exh: Chenil Gallery, Jan 1911 (7)
National Museum of Wales, Cardiff

Gill showed this work and two more mother and child groups
(see *cat.3*) at his first exhibition (shared with the painter
J.D.Innes) at the Chenil Gallery, King's Road, Chelsea, in January 1911. All were carved during 1910. The *Times* critic
decided that Gill had tried to 'express the instinct of maternity'
and Roger Fry wrote: 'has anyone ever looked more directly
at the real thing and seen its pathetic animalism as Gill has?
Merely to have seen what the gesture of pressing the breast
with the left hand means, as he has, seems to be a piece of deep
imagination.' Gill's wife Ethel Mary had given birth to their
third daughter Joanna in February 1910 and that event could
well have inspired Gill. However, the child in the arms of this
mother is male, unlike Gill's own baby, and imparts a covert
Christian message to this pagan earthly group.

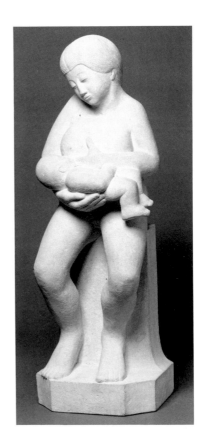

3 Mother and Child

1910

Portland stone, $34 \times 10\frac{3}{4} \times 8\frac{3}{4}$ in / $86.4 \times 27.3 \times 22.2$ cm

Exh: Chenil Gallery, Jan 1911 (1)

The Provost and Scholars of King's College, Cambridge

This work is unfinished and only carved down from the top to a depth of 11 inches. The title Gill used when he exhibited it in 1911 reveals that it was intended to be a mother and child group. What is visible is the mother's head, shoulders and left arm, which holds her breast ready for her child. (For a finished version of this subject, see *cat.2*.) Maynard Keynes visited Gill's first solo exhibition at the Chenil Gallery, London and admired this sculpture. John Knewstub, owner of the Gallery, wrote to Keynes stating that Gill had meant to finish this work but had been very busy prior to the opening of the show. Gill was prepared to accept Keynes's offer of £25 for the stone as it was, in its unfinished state. A further letter from Knewstub to Keynes then offered an alternative response by Gill, who wished to carry on with the sculpture: 'It is wholly contrary to him to leave his work unfinished and he could derive no satisfaction in disposing of his work in that state. It is his intention to carry the *Mother and Child* somewhat further, but it will differ wholly from the other two on view here – the price when finished will be £45.' In the event it was left unfinished and Gill charged Keynes £25 for the sculpture.

4 A Roland for an Oliver

1910

Hoptonwood stone relief with added colour –
gilded necklace, red lips and nipples, $37\frac{1}{4} \times 27\frac{1}{8} \times 5\frac{1}{4}$ in /
$94.6 \times 68 \times 13.3$ cm

Inscr: O PALE GALILEAN. BUT THESE / THOU SHALT NOT TAKE: THE LAUREL / THE PALM & THE PAEAN THE / BREASTS OF THE NYMPHS IN THE BRAKE and with symbol of an eye in a hand, on back

Exh: Chenil Gallery, Jan 1911 (11)

The University of Hull Art Collection

The phrase 'A Roland for an Oliver' is another way of saying 'tit for tat', implying an evenly matched conflict. It refers to the pairing of this relief of a seductive nude female with a relief of the crucified and naked Christ (see *cat.6*). Gill worked on this sculpture between 4 January and 2 September 1910, spending thirty-two days on the carving and four days cutting the inscription. The text on the raised border is taken from lines 23-4 and 35 from Swinburne's poem 'Hymn to Proserpine'. Both this relief and *Crucifixion* (*cat.6*) were exhibited together, hung side by side, at Gill's first exhibition and both were priced at £100 each, by far the highest values in the exhibition. Roger Fry and Robert Ross, as officers for the newly formed Contemporary Art Society, bought both reliefs for their society, the first sculptures to be purchased.

See ill. p.27

  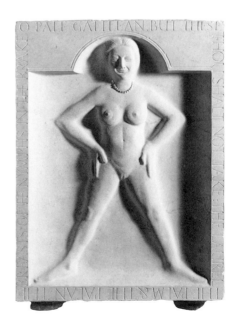

5 Design for Sculpture: A Roland for an Oliver

1910

Pencil with yellow crayon, squared for transfer

33 × 18½ in / 84 × 47 cm

Inscr: LA JOIE DE / VIVRE

Austin Desmond & Phipps

This preparatory drawing is the design for the female figure in the relief *A Roland for an Oliver* (cat.4). It is full-size and is translated into stone virtually without alteration, except for the loss of the title '*La Joie de Vivre*' set between the figure's legs, and the addition of a necklace. In the design the figure's hair assumes more of a sharp halo-like form than it does in the carved relief, where the hair merges into the background plane.

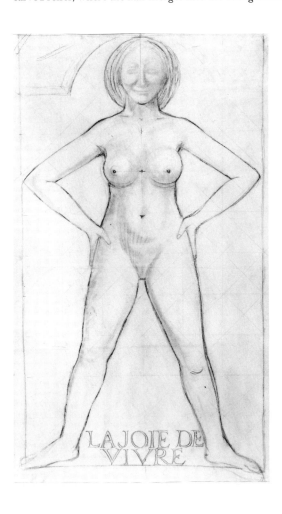

6 Crucifixion

1910

Hoptonwood stone relief with added colour, 37¼ × 30¼ × 5 in / 94.6 × 78.1 × 12.7 cm

Inscr: NEC.IN.TIBIIS.VIRI/BENEPLACITUM.ERIT.EI and ΚΑΙ ΕΙΣΙΝ / ΕΥΝΟΥΧΟΙ / ΟΙΤΙΝΕΣ / ΕΥΝΟΥΧΙΣ / ΑΝ ΕΑΥΤΟ / ΥΣ ΔΙΑ ΤΗΝ / ΒΑΣΙΛΕΙΑΝ / ΤΩΝ ΟΥΡΑ / ΝΩΝ / Ο ΔΥΝΑΜΕ / ΝΟΣΧΩΡΕ / ΙΝΧΩΡΕΙΤΩ with symbol of an eye in a hand, on back

Exh: Chenil Gallery, Jan 1911 (10);

Tate Gallery, presented by the Contemporary Art Society, 1920

Gill's diary for 1910 reveals that he worked on this relief from 17 January until 3 March, and his working title for it was '*Schmerz*'. He spent twenty-six days carving it. The companion piece to this (cat.4) had a working title of '*Joie*'. The raised Greek letters, which are set out horizontally, are taken from St Matthew, 19, v.12. The incised Latin letters, set vertically in the upright shaft of the cross, are taken from Psalm 147, v.10. When the Contemporary Art Society gave this relief to the Tate Gallery in 1920, it was the first work by Gill to enter the national collections.

See ill. p.26

7 Ecstasy

1910–11
Portland stone relief, 54 × 18 × 9 in / 137.2 × 45.7 × 22.8 cm
Inscr: with symbol of an eye in a hand, on r. edge
Tate Gallery

Gill worked on this relief between 5 August 1910 and 2 January 1911. His working title for it was 'They – (big)' to distinguish it from a work of the same title, and presumably the same subject, called 'They – (small)', which was begun on 2 August 1910. This latter work is probably the relief known as *Votes for Women* (see p.29). It is believed that Gill's sister Gladys and her first husband Ernest Laughton provided him with the inspiration for both works. *Ecstasy* (it only gained this title after Gill's death) was bought from Gill by Edward Perry Warren on 23 April 1912 for £60. Warren lived in style in Lewes, Sussex, and collected Greek and Roman sculpture. In 1904 he commissioned from Rodin a marble group of *The Kiss* (now in the Tate Gallery), so with the acquisition of this work by Gill, he owned two unexhibitable sculptures with sexual intercourse as their subject.
See ill. p.52

Photograph before damage
to top left corner

8 Design for Sculpture: Ecstasy

1910
Pencil on tracing paper, squared for transfer
9½ × 5½ in / 24.2 × 14 cm
Inscr: 1910
The Trustees of the British Museum

The date on this sheet looks as though it was written at a different time from the numbers which mark the grid of squares. And if the drawing does relate to the carved stone relief (*cat. 7*), the figures in the carving adopt a different pose, especially their legs and heads. The figures in this drawing are quite close in design to those in a wood engraving of *Lovers*, which Gill cut in 1924 [P293].

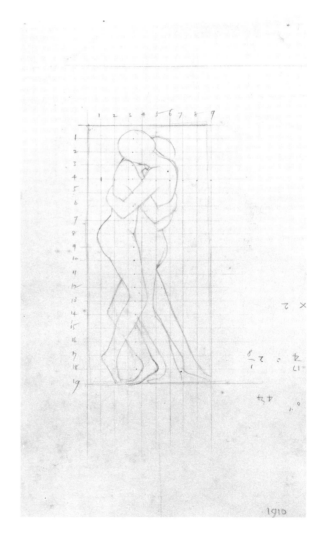

9 Rubbing of Sculpture: Lovers
1921
Wax crayon on paper, $13\frac{3}{4} \times 7\frac{1}{2}$ in / 35 × 19 cm
Inscr: *Corsham stone EG 9.3. '21'*
The Trustees of the British Museum

The present whereabouts of the sculpture from which this rubbing was taken is unknown. It is another example of the theme of human love-making which occupied Gill throughout his career.

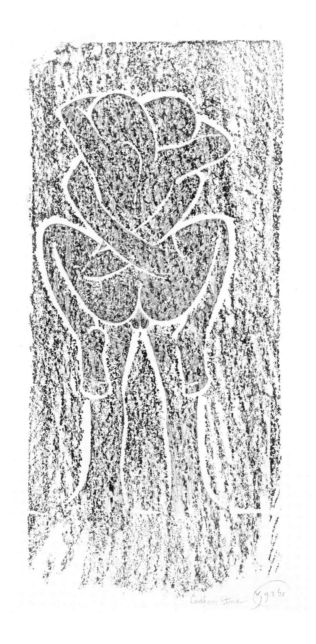

10 The Golden Calf

1912
Hoptonwood stone with added colour, originally gilded
17 × 22 × 8 in / 42 × 55.5 × 20.5 cm
Exh : Second Post-Impressionist Exhibition, Grafton Galleries,
5 Oct – 31 Dec 1912 (21)
Art Collection, Harry Ransom Humanities Research Center,
The University of Texas at Austin (885)

Gill met Madame Strindberg, the widow of the playwright, on 7 May 1912, to discuss plans for the decoration of her new nightclub, the Cabaret Theatre Club, situated in a basement at 9 Heddon Street, off Regent Street. The alternative title for the club was The Cave of the Calf, and this was a reference to the golden calf which the Israelites set up as an object of pagan worship while in the wilderness. Madame Strindberg intended that the atmosphere of her club would equal the orgiastic revelry of the Israelites. Gill was asked to make a sculpture of a golden calf as a central feature of the club's decorations, and he worked on this from 22 May until 8 July 1912. He spent an evening at the club, along with William Rothenstein, on 4 July. On 29 July he made enquiries in Brighton about the gilding of the animal. Because the club was in financial difficulties from the time of its opening, it seems that *The Golden Calf* never reached its destined place there. Instead it was shown in Fry's second Post-Impressionist Exhibition between October and December 1912, and then in February 1913 transferred from the Grafton Galleries to the Goupil Gallery for storage.
C. K. Butler, a prominent member of the Contemporary Art Society, bought it from the Goupil Gallery. Gill also designed the membership cards, the menu stands and a carved and painted relief for the club, all showing the calf in profile. The carved relief was set in the wall by the entrance.

11 Madonna and Child

1912
Portland stone relief with added colour
$18\frac{1}{2} \times 8\frac{1}{2} \times 3$ in / $47 \times 21.4 \times 7.6$ cm
Inscr: E / G with an incised shape of a fish between the letters,
on the left side of the base
Art Collection, Harry Ransom Humanities Research Center,
The University of Texas at Austin (886)

Throughout his career, Gill painted examples of his sculpture,
whether sacred or secular. This appears to be the first time he
applied paint to a stone carving of the Madonna and Child. He
applied red paint to the lips of the two figures, and to the
Madonna's nipples, just as he had done with the sensual female
in *A Roland for an Oliver* (cat.4). Both the Madonna and the
Christ child have gilded hair suggesting an aureole. The plain
base with its raised edge looks as though it could have carried
a lettered inscription. The image of the Madonna and Child
combined with an inscription is found in a wood engraving
of 1914 (see cat.12). This relief was first owned by Lawrence
Dale, the architect of St Alban's Roman Catholic Church,
Oxford, for which Gill provided an incised set of Stations of
the Cross in 1938.
See ill. p.51

12 Madonna and Child

1914
Wood engraving, $12\frac{5}{8} \times 6\frac{1}{4}$ in / 32×16 cm
Inscr: + ET VERBUM / CARO FACTUM / EST.ET HABITA- / VIT.IN
NOBIS in reverse
City Museum and Art Gallery, Stoke-on-Trent

This wood engraving [P27] is listed in Gill's diary as the first
to be cut 'on plank', from a piece of pear wood. Only a handful
of prints were taken from it because Gill filled the cut lines with
gesso and then sent it for display, as an object, to his friend
Everard Meynell's bookshop in London. This gessoed block is
now in the collection of the William Andrews Clark Memorial
Library, Los Angeles. The pose of the Madonna suckling the
child is the same as that found in cats.2 and 11.

13 Madonna and Child

1912–13
Plaster cast, painted, $7\frac{1}{2} \times 2 \times 2\frac{1}{4}$ in / $19 \times 5.1 \times 5.8$ cm
Inscr: EG 67 on base
Exh: Goupil Gallery, Jan 1914 (6)
Manchester City Art Galleries

Gill modelled this small group of the *Madonna and Child* in
plasticine in 1912. In January 1913 he had it transferred into
plaster by a London firm of casters, Broad, Salmon and Co of
41–2 Windmill Street. He worked for a day on the plaster cast
and then this was taken back to Broads to be cast into an edition
in bronze. For some reason Gill was not happy with the bronze
edition made by Broads and in February he chose another casting firm in London, Charles Smith & Sons, Sculptors' Moulders,
of 1 Southcote Road, Holloway, to make a plaster edition. It
seems he had a dozen plaster casts made at a time, and the full
extent of the plaster edition is not known. The plaster casts
were sold for £1. 0. 0 each. This cast from Manchester has the
inscription 'EG 67' written on its base and the number could
indicate its edition number. Each plaster group was decorated
in a different way. Another plaster cast from the same original
is in the William Andrews Clark Memorial Library, Los
Angeles, and the Madonna wears a blue dress with a plum and
gold headdress. A bronze cast of this group is in the collection
of Johannesburg Art Gallery.

14 Madonna and Child

1912–13
Bronze, $6\frac{1}{8} \times 2 \times 1\frac{3}{4}$ in / $15.6 \times 5.1 \times 4.4$ cm
Inscr: Eric Gill No 3 on base
Manchester City Art Galleries

Gill modelled this group during 1912, probably again using
plasticine. In 1913 he had it cast into a plaster edition by
Charles Smith & Sons (see cat. 15), and a bronze edition by
Alex Parlanti, Bronze Founder, 59 Parsons Green Lane, Fulham.
This group of Madonna and Child has less of the Christian trap-
pings of the pair seen in cat. 13, because this mother figure is
only clothed below the waist, and does not have a crown and
veil. Charles Rutherston bought this cast from Gill and it is
inscribed with 'Eric Gill No 3' on its base. A larger stone version of this group, $19\frac{1}{4}$ in (49 cm) high, is in the collection
of the Harry Ransom Humanities Research Center, The University of Texas at Austin, no.911.

15 Madonna and Child

1912–13
Plaster cast, painted, $6\frac{1}{8} \times 2 \times 1\frac{3}{4}$ in / 15.6 × 5.1 × 4.4 cm
Victor Arwas

This is a plaster version of the bronze *Madonna and Child*
(cat.14).

16 Madonna and Child

1913
Plaster cast, painted, $6\frac{1}{2} \times 2\frac{1}{2} \times 2$ in / 16.5 × 6.3 × 5.1 cm
Inscr: EG 36 on base
West Sussex Record Office, Eric Gill Collection no.294

On 4 August 1913, Gill recorded in his diary: 'Plasticine model
of our Lady & child (ie. altering M&C 2 – putting clothes on
& crown etc, also feet)'. He thus converted the simplified
group of cats 14 and 15 into a more regal *Madonna and Child*
again, so that it bears comparison with cat.13. Mary, although
still with bare breasts, wears a long robe and a crown and veil.
Gill took the plasticine original on 16 August to Smith & Sons
to be cast into a plaster edition. This cast has 'EG 36' on its
base, and the painted decoration is believed to have been done
by Desmond Chute.

17 The Rower

1912
Hoptonwood stone, 10 × 11 × 2 in / 25.6 × 28 × 5.1 cm
Douglas Woolf

Gill worked on this figure from 11 to 31 October 1912, and
on the day of its completion he had it professionally photographed, placed in two separate positions. One shows the
figure balancing on its feet and the other shows it rotated
through ninety degrees, in a seated position (see p.32). The latter position is the source for its witty title. Gill made more than
one sculpture with a dual orientation as here, and again the
sculpture was of a naked acrobatic figure (cat.25). He liked to
draw attention to ideas about balance. Concurrent with the
making of this sculpture, Gill had three small stone sculptures
of naked acrobats on exhibition in Roger Fry's second Post-
Impressionist Exhibition. *The Rower* was bought from Gill by
C.K.Butler, who also bought the *The Golden Calf* (cat.10).

18 Crucifixion

1913
Hoptonwood stone relief – letters painted red
$17\frac{3}{4} \times 6\frac{3}{4} \times 1\frac{1}{2}$ in / 45.5 × 17.5 × 3.8 cm
Inscr : O TE FELICEM
Exh : Goupil Gallery, Jan 1914 (10)
Tate Gallery

Gill's diary for 1913 records that he carved this crucifixion in Hoptonwood stone between 18 April and 7 July. He carved another crucifixion in incised marble during the same period. The subject of the crucifixion was the one that occupied Gill most during his career, both from personal choice and through public commissions, especially tombstones and memorials. The figure of Christ in this relief is slim, with puny legs, which resemble the insignificant legs of the Christ on Gill's first relief of the Crucifixion, in 1910 (*cat* 6). Christ's right hand is held in a gesture of benediction, and this is found again on several more works by Gill : *cat*.19 ; the Twelfth and the Fourteenth Stations of the Cross in Westminster Cathedral, 1914-18 ; and two wood engravings [P 15 and P 16], cut in 1913. The latter is *cat*.20. The inscription on this relief, 'O TE FELICEM', is not a biblical quotation, but rather a personal note from Gill. The English translation of the inscription reads 'O Happy Thou', and it must refer to the viewer who realises that he or she is blessed and redeemed by the love of Christ. The letters of the inscription are painted red.

19 Design for Sculpture : Crucifixion

1912
Pencil and watercolour, $11\frac{3}{4} \times 7\frac{1}{8}$ in / 29.8 × 18.1 cm
National Museum of Wales, Cardiff

Gill carved a number of small crucifixes in 1913 and this drawing is similar in form to a small stone relief of the subject, also with a rounded top, whose present whereabouts are unknown.

20 Crucifixion

1913
Wood engraving (3rd state), $7\frac{1}{8} \times 2\frac{3}{4}$ in / 18.1 × 7 cm
City Museum and Art Gallery, Stoke-on-Trent

This wood engraving [P16], cut in 1913, is close in design to
the carved stone relief (cat. 18). The pose of Christ and his
gesture of benediction are the same, but the print does not have
the inscription at the foot of the cross. Christopher Skelton
states that the wooden block from which a similar engraving
[P15] was cut was offered for sale as a religious object at
Everard Meynell's bookshop in London (see also cat. 12).

21 Boxers

1913
Portland stone relief, with added colour
$22 \times 19\frac{1}{2} \times 7\frac{3}{4}$ in / 55.8 × 49.5 × 19.7 cm
Exh: Goupil Gallery, Jan 1914 (3 at £42.0.0)
Stephen Keynes

This relief was carved between 16 May and 3 July 1913. Gill's
diary entry for 13 May states 'Kessler Acrobat & Boxers – drawings', so it seems likely that Count Harry Kessler had commissioned sculptures of both subjects. Gill treats the relief as
though it were a metope from a Greek temple, setting a pair
of figures in action within a plain architectural frame. It was
shown at the Goupil Gallery in January 1914 in an unpainted
state. At some time between then and March 1915 Gill painted
the relief, making one figure yellow, the other red, the background green, and the architectural frame blue. Geoffrey
Keynes wished to buy it in March 1915 as a wedding present
for his friend George Mallory, but was not pleased to discover
it had been painted. It was thought unwise to try to remove
the colour, and the relief was sold to Keynes for £20. It would
appear therefore that Count Kessler did not buy the relief, even
though he commissioned it. In 1937 Gill carved another relief
of two boxers, as part of his architectural decorations for the
façade of the People's Palace, Mile End.

22 Design for Sculpture: Boxers

1913

Pencil and watercolour, $4\frac{7}{8} \times 4\frac{7}{8}$ in / 12.4 × 12.4 cm

Inscr: EG 13.5.13

Exh: *Drawings & Engravings by Eric Gill*, Alpine Club Gallery, 5–14 May 1918 (91)

Art Collection, Harry Ransom Humanities Research Center, The University of Texas at Austin (941)

This is one of the preparatory drawings that Gill made for his relief *Boxers* (cat.21), commissioned by Count Kessler. Although he exhibited the stone relief unpainted, the drawing shows the figures of the boxers coloured red and yellow as they were eventually to become. The drawing also shows the boxers wearing gloves, but these are omitted from the carving.

23 Design for Sculpture: Boxers

1913

Pencil, squared for transfer, $18\frac{3}{4} \times 20\frac{1}{2}$ in / 47.5 × 52 cm

Mr and Mrs Graham Howes

This full-scale drawing shows the composition of the *Boxers* relief (cat.21) as it was actually carved. Drawings of clenched fists, taken no doubt from life, and probably Gill's own hand, are added to the sheet.

24 Rubbing of Sculpture: Woman

1912
Wax crayon on paper, 30 × 15 in / 76.2 × 38.1 cm
Inscr: *30 Apr 1912 rubbing of drawing in stone £5. 5. 0* on verso
The Trustees of the British Museum

On 30 April 1912 Gill's diary records that he spent three hours cutting an outline in stone of a naked woman, and he titled the work 'Gladys'. This rubbing is taken from the incised outline on the same day that Gill carved it. The stone's present whereabouts are unknown. Gladys was the name of Gill's sister, who had provided him with the inspiration for earlier sculptures, *Ecstasy* (cat.7) and *Votes for Women* (see cat.7, and p.29). It seems as though she was his early role model of a sensual woman, and he liked to portray her in acrobatic poses. With her knees drawn up close to her body, the female figure in this rubbing adopts a pose similar to that found in the female acrobat in cat.25.

25 Design for Sculpture: Acrobat

1913
Pencil, watercolour, black ink and crayon, squared for transfer
14¾ × 9¾ in / 37.5 × 24.8 cm
Inscr: *EG 15.5.13*
The Fine Art Society plc, London

Gill's diary records on 15 May 'Kessler Acrobat – Boxers drawings', so this drawing of a naked female acrobat was made in response to a commission from Count Kessler. The drawing is the same size as the carved sculpture (8¾ × 6 in / 22.2 × 15.2 cm), which was made from Bath stone and balanced on its feet. It is now only known through photographs. In 1927 it was owned by Mr Cosmo Gordon, so perhaps it did not reach Count Kessler's collection.

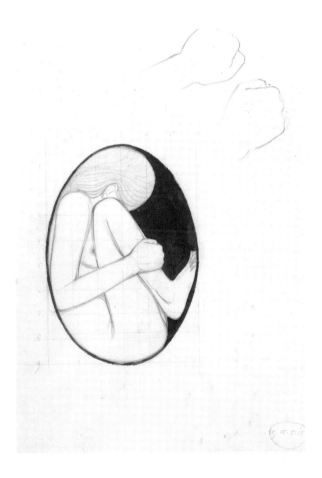

26 Rubbing of Sculpture: Acrobat

1913
Wax crayon on paper, $10 \times 7\frac{1}{2}$ in / 25.4 × 19.1 cm
Private collection

This is a rubbing taken from a carved preparatory outline on one face of a block of Bath stone from which Gill then carved the complete sculpture of a small naked female acrobat. The drawing for the sculpture is *cat*.25. The acrobat was reproduced in both Rothenstein, pl.12 (see below), and Thorp, pl.4.

27 Design for Sculpture: Acrobat

1915
Pencil and crayon, squared for transfer
$10\frac{3}{4} \times 13$ in / 27.3 × 33 cm
Inscr: *Raffalovich Acrobat* II f.S. E.G. *July* 1915
Sandra Lummis Fine Art, London

This drawing is a full-scale study for the stone figure of a naked male acrobat, *Acrobat* no.2, which Gill carved for André Raffalovich intermittently between 26 July and 3 October 1915. Its present whereabouts are unknown. Gill and Raffalovich met at the latter's house in Edinburgh on 26 June 1914, and quickly became good friends. By 17 July Raffalovich had deposited £280 in Gill's bank account in respect of commissioning two sculptures of acrobats, and a sculpture of St Sebastian (*cat*.38). Gill carved *Acrobat* no.1 for Raffalovich between 9 June and 9 August from a piece of alabaster. Like *Acrobat* no.2, it is also lost.

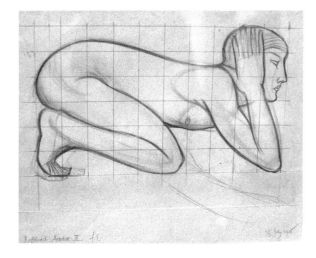

28 Design for Sculpture: Fifth Station of the Cross, Westminster Cathedral

1913

Pencil, ink and wash, $5 \times 5\frac{1}{4}$ in / 12.7 × 13 cm

Inscr: *The fifth Station, Simon of Cyrene helps Jesus to carry the Cross* +

Manchester City Art Galleries

Gill provisionally gained the commission to carve the fourteen Stations of the Cross for Westminster Cathedral, but was required, at his own expense, to provide a trial panel, 4 feet 6 inches square. If the Cathedral authorities approved this trial panel, then he would be permitted to proceed with the whole set of fourteen. Gill chose the Fifth Station as his trial panel, and this is the second of the preliminary designs for it, which he drew in December 1913. The stone trial relief keeps close to the drawing; it is made from Hoptonwood stone, was carved during January and February 1914, and is now in the collection of the Harry Ransom Humanities Research Center, The University of Texas at Austin (887). The drawing was given to the City Art Gallery, Manchester by Charles Rutherston. When Gill carved the larger Fifth Station of the Cross for Westminster Cathedral, he reversed the composition.

29 The Fourteen Stations of the Cross

1917

Wood engravings, each 3 × 3 in / 7.6 × 7.6 cm

Ronald A. B. Sim, The Bloomsbury Workshop

On 15 April 1917, with over half of the Westminster Cathedral Stations of the Cross carved, Gill discussed with his assistant Ralph Beedham the production of a small book of wood engravings based on his Stations. The book was published by the St Dominic's Press, Ditchling in 1917 with the title *The Way of the Cross*. The fourteen Stations of the Cross are:

1. Jesus is condemned to death
2. Jesus receives His Cross
3. Jesus falls the first time
4. Jesus meets His Mother
5. Simon of Cyrene helps Jesus to carry the Cross
6. Jesus meets Veronica
7. Jesus falls the second time
8. Jesus speaks to the women of Jerusalem
9. Jesus falls the third time
10. Jesus is stripped
11. Jesus is nailed to the Cross
12. Jesus dies upon the Cross (below)
13. The Body of Jesus is taken down from the Cross
14. The Body of Jesus is laid in the tomb

30 Design for Seventh Station of the Cross, Westminster Cathedral

1916
Pencil and yellow crayon, squared for transfer
28½ × 29¾ in / 72.4 × 75.6 cm
Inscr: EG Dec 4 1916
The Board of Trustees of the Victoria and Albert Museum,
London E3001-1923

The subject of the Seventh Station is 'Jesus falls the second time'. This half full-size drawing shows the design as it was eventually carved, a job which occupied Gill from 13 June to 16 October 1917. A bearded onlooker helps Christ steady the cross while a Roman soldier keeps control of Christ by a rope tied around his waist.

31 Design for Seventh Station of the Cross, Westminster Cathedral

1916
Pencil, yellow, blue, pink and orange crayon, squared for transfer
28½ × 29¾ in / 72.4 × 75.6 cm
Inscr: EG 4.12.'16
The Board of Trustees of the Victoria and Albert Museum,
London E3002-1923

This half full-size drawing, executed on the same day as cat.30, indicates only the contours of the shapes to be cut in the stone relief. Four background areas are shaded yellow, blue, pink and orange and these four colours indicate the different depths of cutting, with blue the deepest, probably one inch, then orange, then yellow, with pink the shallowest level.

VII. JESUS FALLS A SECOND TIME.

The relief as executed

32 Design for Twelfth Station of the Cross, Westminster Cathedral

1917
Pencil, ink and watercolour, squared for transfer
$28\frac{1}{2} \times 29\frac{3}{4}$ in / 72.4 × 75.6 cm
Inscr: *EG Sept 7.'17*
The Board of Trustees of the Victoria and Albert Museum, London E3011-1923

The subject of the Twelfth Station of the Cross is 'Jesus dies upon the Cross'. The state of this half full-size drawing, with two areas of paper cut away, indicates that Gill changed his mind about the composition of this Station during the execution of this drawing. It shows that he originally envisaged Mary at the side of the Cross, and she is omitted in the relief as carved. Gill worked on the stone relief between 15 February and 26 March 1918.

33 Design for Twelfth Station of the Cross, Westminster Cathedral

1917
Pencil, blue, orange and yellow crayon, squared for transfer
$28\frac{1}{2} \times 29\frac{3}{4}$ in / 72.4 × 75.6 cm
Inscr: *EG 25.10.'17*
The Board of Trustees of the Victoria and Albert Museum, London E3012-1923

This half full-size drawing indicates only the contours of the shapes to be cut in the stone relief. Areas of the design are shaded with orange, yellow and blue and Gill indicates on this design that the orange areas are to be cut to a depth of half an inch, blue one inch and yellow 'various'. David Jones, in his appreciation of Gill as a sculptor, published shortly after Gill's death, singled out his Westminster Stations of the Cross as 'a unique achievement' and added 'No.12 in particular has great feeling and is a true ikon'.

The relief as executed

34 Design for Sculpture: Fourteenth Station of the Cross, St Cuthbert's Church, Bradford

1921

Pen and ink, $4\frac{3}{4} \times 4\frac{3}{4}$ in / 12.1 × 12.1 cm

Inscr: *Desmond Chute, 1921, Design for XIVth Station, Bradford*

West Sussex Record Office, Eric Gill Collection no.231

Gill's good friend, Father John O'Connor, priest of St Cuthbert's Church, Wilmer Road, Heaton, Bradford (from 1919 to 1952), asked for a set of Stations of the Cross for his own church, following the critical success of the Westminster Cathedral Stations. Gill asked Desmond Chute to help him with the designs and this small drawing for the Fourteenth Station – 'The Body of Jesus is laid in the tomb' – is from Chute's hand. The carved relief remains close to the drawing, which is based on William Blake's tempera painting *The Procession from Calvary*, in the collection of the Tate Gallery. Blake was an artist greatly admired by both Chute and Gill. Gill carved the Bradford Stations between 1921 and 1924. They are of Beer stone and are 30 inches square (76.2 cm). Gill made two further sets of Stations of the Cross, the first for the Roman Catholic Church of Our Lady and St Peter, Garlands Road, Leatherhead, in 1922–3, and the second for the Roman Catholic Church of St Alban, Charles Street, Oxford, from 1938 to 1940.

35 Gingerbread Madonna and Child

1919–20

Corsham stone, $13\frac{3}{4} \times 6\frac{3}{4} \times 2\frac{3}{4}$ in / 35 × 17.1 × 7 cm

West Sussex Record Office, Eric Gill Collection no. 296

In the Autumn of 1919 Elizabeth Gill, then aged fourteen, drew a picture of the Madonna and Child. As on other occasions, Gill converted one of his daughter's drawings into a sculpture, which gained the delightful title of the *Gingerbread Madonna and Child*. Gill carved the sculpture between 20 December 1919 and 28 January 1920 and it was purchased by Desmond Chute in July 1920 for £5. For Gill's own preliminary drawing for this work (see *cat.36*). He also used Elizabeth's drawing as the basis for a wood engraving (*cat.37*).

36 Design for Sculpture: Gingerbread Madonna and Child

1919

Pencil, $9\frac{1}{4} \times 6\frac{1}{8}$ in / 23.5 × 15.6 cm

Inscr: *Gingerbread M & C EG 20.12.19*

Art Collection, Harry Ransom Humanities Research Center, The University of Texas at Austin (955)

This drawing is for *cat.35*, the Corsham stone *Gingerbread Madonna and Child*.

37 Madonna and Child with Base

1919

Wood engraving, $2\frac{3}{4} \times 2$ in / 7 × 5.1 cm

City Museum and Art Gallery, Stoke-on-Trent

This wood engraving [P155] is related to both *cats 35 and 36*. It was first published in vol.III, no. 2 of the periodical *The Game*, published by the St Dominic's Press, Ditchling, for Advent 1919, and then Gill pulled some prints of it for use as Christmas cards that same year.

38 St Sebastian

1919–20
Portland stone, 41 × 8 × 10 in / 104 × 20.3 × 25.4 cm
Exh: Victoria and Albert Museum, Jan 1941 (no catalogue)
Tate Gallery

Gill did drawings for this sculpture on 28 and 29 March and
1 April 1919. It was commissioned from André Raffalovich,
who had earlier asked Gill to make him two small stone acrobats (see *cat. 27*). Gill carved this figure intermittently between
6 June 1919 and 1 April 1920. It was dispatched to Raffalovich
in Edinburgh and was in his possession by 16 June 1920. Gill
wrote on that date to Raffalovich: 'You will be amused to hear
that the study from which I did the carving was made from
myself in a mirror. I think the chest and arm-pits are the best
part certainly. I think the head is good though not, perhaps,
in quite the same style. The tree is rather out of keeping being
much more conventional than the figure. I think the legs are
the weak part, at any rate from the knees downwards.' Gill
carved another figure of St Sebastian from Bath stone in 1927
and produced a wood engraving of the saint in 1922 [P200].
See ill. p.53

39 Design for Sculpture: St Sebastian

1919
Pencil on tracing paper, 10¾ × 8¾ in / 27.4 × 22.3 cm
Inscr: S *Sebastian* EG 29...
Art Collection, Harry Ransom Humanities Research Center,
The University of Texas at Austin (957)

This is a preliminary drawing for *cat.38*. The date is incomplete
on the drawing, but it is likely to be the one Gill made on 29
March 1919.

40 The Bath

1920
Beer stone, double relief, with added colour
8 × 6½ × 3¾ in / 20.3 × 16.5 × 1.9 cm
Exh: Goupil Gallery Salon, Nov–Dec 1920 (377 at £20)
Private collection
courtesy The Fine Art Society plc, London

This work initiates a new genre in Gill's sculpture, that of the
double relief. Sculptures of this kind are fully in the round but
very narrow in depth. *The Bath* was exhibited in 1920 along
with two other double relief sculptures: *The Couch*, a similar
subject (present whereabouts unknown) and *Adam and Eve*,
two naked torsos (collection William Andrews Clark Memorial
Library, Los Angeles). The model for this sculpture is believed
to have been Petra, Gill's daughter, then aged fourteen.

41 Girl in the Bath II

1923
Wood engraving, 4 × 4 in / 10.2 × 10.2 cm
City Museum and Art Gallery, Stoke-on-Trent

This wood engraving [P218], like cat.40, was also inspired by
Petra Gill, and makes a feature of the fall of her long hair.

42 Headless Female Torso

1920
Bath stone, $16\frac{1}{8} \times 8 \times 2\frac{3}{4}$ in / 41 × 20.3 × 7 cm
Art Collection, Harry Ransom Humanities Research Center,
The University of Texas at Austin (891)

This appears to be the first example of a figure by Gill which
omits the head and part of the limbs. He had made a tentative
step in this direction with an armless nude female figure carved
between 1913 and 1915, Torso with Head (illustrated in Thorp,
pl.7). By deciding not to include the head and by only showing
the figure down to the thighs, Gill has here concentrated on
the anatomy of the female torso and introduced a mood of
sensuality. He was to present a headless female torso again, in
his large sculpture Mankind, 1927–8 (cat.76), and on a much
smaller scale, in 1924 (see cat.61).

43 Model for Sculpture: Christ, Leeds University War Memorial

1922

Caen stone relief, $26\frac{1}{4} \times 13\frac{5}{8} \times 4$ in / $66.6 \times 34.5 \times 10.2$ cm

Inscr: JDPONIIIIID/DIXIT JESUS on verso

Art Collection, Harry Ransom Humanities Research Center, The University of Texas at Austin (894)

By 1917 Gill was in receipt of a major commission from Professor Michael Sadler of Leeds University to carve a large relief as a memorial to those members of Leeds University who had been killed in the First World War. The subject agreed on was Gill's own choice, 'Christ Driving out the Money Changers from the Temple'. Gill spent from 4 to 11 January 1922 carving this scale model of the figure of Christ wielding his whip, one-third of the full size, 'so as to acquaint myself with the problem and to discover the amount of relief required (Result: $4\frac{1}{2}''$ relief for figures about 4' 6" high)' (letter to Desmond Chute, 18 February 1922). The pose of Christ is much the same as that on the memorial (cat. 44), but the naked male figure at the feet of Christ in this model is replaced by a Mother and Child group.

¶ Another model for the figure of Christ exists, in the collection of the William Andrews Clark Memorial Library, Los Angeles. It is similar in size to cat.43 but is in the round and has applied colour. It shows Christ holding his whip in his hands while treading on a top hat and a bag spilling gold coins. Beside Christ a book lies open, with the inscription 'LEGES/LATRON/UM', and He stands on a lettered base: 'AGITE/NUNC/DIVITES'. The latter quotation is taken from St James, 5, v.1.

44 Leeds University War Memorial:
Christ Driving out the Money Changers from the
Temple
1922–3
Portland stone, $66\frac{5}{8} \times 192 \times 8\frac{7}{8}$ in / 169.1 × 481.1 × 22.6 cm
Inscr:
along cornice: AGITE NUNC, DIVITES, PLORATE ULULANTES IN
MISERIIS VESTRIS, QUAE ADVENIENT VOBIS. DIVITIAE VESTRAE
PUTREFACTAE SUNT
in panel above dog: -ET CUM FECISSET / QUASI FLAGELLUM / DE
FUNICULIS, OMNES EJECIT / DE TEMPLO, ET NUMULARI / ORUM
EFFUDIT AES, ET MEN / SAS SUBVERTIT. ET DIXIT : / NOLITE FACERE
DOMUM / PATRIS MEI DOMUM / NEGOTIATIONIS
University of Leeds (represented by photographs)

Although Sadler had given Gill the commission for this war memorial in 1917, work on it was not begun in earnest until 1922. It was a project that greatly excited Gill, for he wrote to William Rothenstein in November 1919 that it was to be 'a magnum opus. I hope it may come off. Christ turning the money changers out – such a subject carved upon such a scale would satisfy all my ambitions – both as man and artist.' Gill began to carve the relief on 27 April 1922 and worked on it intermittently until 8 July that year. Then there was a long pause until 5 January 1923 when it occupied most of his time until 23 April. On 4 May he prepared the stones for dispatch to Leeds. The relief was set against the south wall of the old Library, and it was unveiled and dedicated by the Bishop of Ripon on 1 June. Response to it was mixed, with some criticism of the figures in contemporary dress. Gill wrote his own pamphlet 'A War Memorial', which put forward his reasons for the choice of subject and his treatment of it. The two inscriptions are from St James, 5, v.1, on the cornice, and the Gospel of St John, 2, vv 15 and 16, in the panel above the dog.

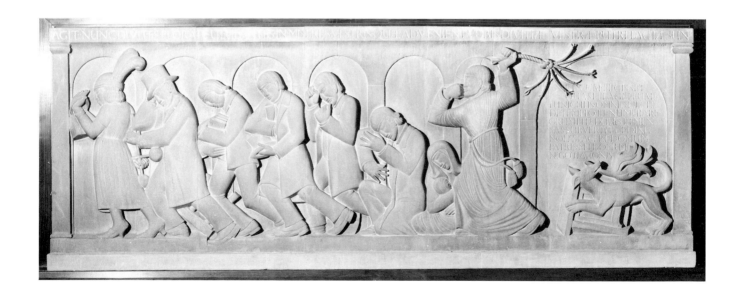

45 Design for Sculpture:
War Memorial of Christ and the Money Changers
1916
Pencil and wash, 19 × 19¼ in / 48.5 × 49 cm
Inscr: ET.INTRAVIT.JESUS.IN.TEMPLUM.DEI.ET.EJICIEBAT / OMNES.
VENDENTES.ET.EMENTES.IN.TEMPLO +
Manchester City Art Galleries

The Civic Arts Association organised a competition in the Summer of 1916 for a large monument to be set up in the new County Hall in memory of London County Council employees killed during the First World War. Gill submitted two drawings, of which this is one (see also *cat.*46), and exhibited both at the RIBA Gallery in July as part of a mixed entry of designs for war memorials. This drawing shows the front elevation of Gill's proposed free-standing figure group in bronze. Gill's design was given second place in the competition 'on the grounds that it did not follow the conditions' (letter to William Rothenstein, 22 July 1916). Gill collaborated with Charles Holden on his entry for this competition and it seems Holden was responsible for the stone plinth. Charles Rutherston bought both of Gill's drawings at the end of 1916 and gave them to the City Art Gallery, Manchester in 1925. The inscription is from the Gospel of St Matthew, 21, v. 12.

46 Design for Sculpture:
War Memorial of Christ and the Money Changers
1916
Pencil and wash, 19 × 19¼ in / 48.5 × 49 cm
Inscr: ET.DICIT.EIS.SCRIPTUM.EST / DOMUS.MEA.DOMUS.
ORATIONIS.VOCABITUR
Manchester City Art Galleries

Along with cat.45, this formed part of Gill's entry to the Civic
Arts Association competition for a war memorial to com-
memorate London County Council employees. It shows the
back elevation of Gill's proposed free-standing figure group in
bronze. The inscription is from the Gospel of St Matthew, 21,
v.13.

47 Christ and the Money Changers
1919
Wood engraving, 2 × 3⅛ in / 5.1 × 7.9 cm
The Bloomsbury Workshop

Gill cut this wood engraving [P152] as an illustration for a
pamphlet on *Riches*, published by St Dominic's Press, Ditchling,
1919. It is very similar to his design for the Civic Arts Association competition (see cat.45). By the end of 1916, Gill had
altered his ideas about the subject of *Christ and the Money
Changers* as a bronze free-standing group, and had begun to
think in terms of a carved stone relief treatment. This wood
engraving treats the subject as though in high relief.

48 Crucifix

1921
Oak, with added colour, 44 × 23 × 3 in / 111.8 × 58.4 × 7.6 cm
Hove Museum and Art Gallery

On 16 June 1920 Gill wrote to André Raffalovich giving him details of the progress of the Ditchling Catholic-based community of which he was the driving force: 'Five of us here are Dominican Tertiaries and we are trying to build a little chapel … We are also proposing to build our workshops in a group in one field and to form a little guild of Christian workmen.' ¶Gill, with his architectural experience, designed the simple chapel which was built by a local bricklayer. It was erected in 1920 in the meadow behind Gill's house, Hopkins Crank, and served as the centre of worship for the Ditchling community, the newly formed Guild of St Joseph and St Dominic, with prayers being said there as often as four times throughout the working day. It ceased to be usable when it was structurally damaged by the hurricane of 1987. The interior was plain whitewashed brick, with two brick buttresses and a wooden tie-beam marking the division between nave and sanctuary. This oak crucifix hung from the beam and functioned as the rood crucifix. Gill began carving it on 8 March and had finished it by 23 March 1921. The following day was spent applying colour and gilding the halo. This is the first crucifix made by Gill to depict Christ wearing the Crown of Thorns.

49 Divine Lovers

1922
Pewter on ebony base, $3\frac{1}{4} \times 2\frac{7}{8} \times \frac{3}{8}$ in / 8.2 × 7.2 × 0.8 cm
Exh: Goupil Gallery Salon, Oct–Dec 1923 (393)
Art Collection, Harry Ransom Humanities Research Center, The University of Texas at Austin (893)

This pewter cast, one of an edition of six, was made from a boxwood original. Gill carved the boxwood group between 27 April and 3 May 1922 and this is now in the Fogg Art Museum, Harvard University, Cambridge, Mass. (see also cat.50). By October 1923 an edition in pewter was announced at £5.5.0 per cast, and Gill gave the work the title of Ikon. The subject of Divine Lovers was one that was central to Gill's thinking; he believed that human love echoed that of Christ the Bridegroom for His Bride, the Church (see also cat.51).
See ill. p.54

50 Divine Lovers I

1922
Wood engraving, $3\frac{1}{2} \times 3$ in / 8.9×7.7 cm
The Bloomsbury Workshop

Gill made two wood engravings on this theme, printing from two separate blocks [P193 and 201]. The second block was engraved and printed, then carved into a free-standing sculpture (see *cat.*49).

51 Nuptials of God

1922
Wood engraving, $2\frac{5}{8} \times 2$ in / 6.5×5.1 cm
City Museum and Art Gallery, Stoke-on-Trent

This arresting image was cut by Gill in 1922 [P214] and used the following year as an illustration in *The Game*, vol. VI, no.34, p.3, published January 1923. It shows the crucified Christ being embraced by a presumably naked female figure, possibly Mary Magdalen. Both have haloes, are holy figures and are meant to symbolise Christ the Bridegroom and his consummated love for the Church, His Bride. Gill was not the only artist to attempt this subject: Rodin carved a small marble group on the same theme in 1894.

52 Madonna and Child

1922
Black slate relief on ebony base
6 × 4 in / 15.2 × 10.2 cm / base 2 × 6 in / 5.1 × 15.2 cm
Ivor Braka Limited, London

Gill carved this small relief between 27 and 29 July 1922. He
rarely used black slate, and this may be a piece of stone from
Wales. The composition of two faces with their profiles
tenderly touching, with eye level with eye, nose with nose and
mouth with mouth, first appears in Gill's work in graphic form
in 1920, with a wood engraving of *Lovers* [P166]. The
engraved figures are seen full-length and naked and the man's
profile appears above the woman's, just as here the Madonna
oversees the Christ child. Gill utilises this composition for five
wood engravings of the *Madonna and Child* [P209, P268, P272,
P286 and P299, executed between 1922 and 1924] and four
further prints of *Lovers*, one of which is entitled *The Soul and
the Bridegroom* [P294, P323, P496 and P835, dating between
1924 and 1932]. This work once belonged to the architect Sir
Edward Maufe, who commissioned Gill to carve a Crucifixion
for the external east wall of his Church of St Thomas the Apostle,
Hanwell, London, in 1937, and also some sculpture for his
new cathedral at Guildford during 1939–40.

53 Madonna and Child : The Shrimp

1922
Wood engraving, $3\frac{1}{2} \times 2\frac{1}{2}$ in / 8.9 × 6.4 cm
The Bloomsbury Workshop

Gill cut this wood engraving [P209] in the Winter of 1922 and
used it as a Christmas card that year. The composition is related
to *cat.*52, although the Madonna's arms adopt a different
posture.

54 Splits I

1923
Beer stone, with added colour
$9\frac{1}{2} \times 22 \times 3\frac{1}{2}$ in / $24 \times 56 \times 9$ cm
Exh: Goupil Gallery Salon, Oct–Dec 1923 (394 at £35.0.0)
Art Collection, Harry Ransom Humanities Research Center,
The University of Texas at Austin (895)

Gill's diaries record that he began carving this work on 1 May
1923, a day on which he was also carving a black marble torso.
The work is not listed in the diary after 5 June 1923, which
is probably its completion date. It marks a return to the theme
of the naked female acrobat, first seen in Gill's work in 1912
(see *cat.17*). This sculpture once belonged to Brinsley Ford,
who became a fervent admirer of Gill's work during the years
1930–3. Ford was an undergraduate at Trinity College, Oxford
in 1930 and his tutor was Stanley Casson, an authority on
Greek sculpture as well as that of his own time. Ford bought
Splits I from Gill in January 1930 and invited him to speak at
Trinity's Debating Society in May 1930.
See ill. p.31

55 Design for Sculpture: Splits I

c.1918
Watercolour on tracing paper
$5\frac{3}{8} \times 9\frac{1}{2}$ in / 13.8×23.7 cm
Inscr: *Top of 'handsome marble clock' carved in beer stone
(with alterations)* 1923. (EG c.1918)
Art Collection, Harry Ransom Humanities Research Center,
The University of Texas at Austin (951[1])

The drawing shows the proposed front face of *Splits I* (*cat.54*).
It is similar to the figure as carved except that in the drawing
the figure places her right arm over her head. There is no
record of Gill designing or carving a 'handsome marble clock'
as the unlikely base for the *Splits I* figure. He did however
design and decorate a wooden clock in 1930, but the decoration consisted entirely of floral motifs.

56 Splits II

1923
Bath stone, with added colour
24¾ × 11 × 4¾ in / 63 × 28 × 12.5 cm
Inscr: EG on right side of base
Exh: Goupil Gallery Salon, Oct–Dec 1923 (395 at £55.0.0)
Art Collection, Harry Ransom Humanities Research Center,
The University of Texas at Austin (896)

This work was executed between 23 August and 1 October
1923. Brinsley Ford, who had purchased *Splits I* (*cat.*54) in
January 1930, persuaded his friends Anthony and Diana
Beaumont to buy this complementary work from Gill in the
same year.
See ill. p.30

57 Study for Sculpture: Splits II

1923
Pencil and watercolour
14⅛ × 6¼ in / 35.9 × 15.9 cm
Art Collection, Harry Ransom Humanities Research Center,
The University of Texas at Austin (965)

58 Study of Medieval Sculpture of Acrobats in Church at Marly-le-Roi

1926
Pencil, 10½ × 8⅛ in / 26.7 × 20.7 cm
Inscr: *at Marly-le-Roi* / 31.5.26
The Trustees of the British Museum

Gill first visited Marly-le-Roi, a Parisian suburb, in January
1910 when he was sent by Count Harry Kessler to meet Maillol,
who lived there. Gill returned to Marly-le-Roi on 31 May 1926,
again to visit Maillol. This drawing appears to be a sketch of
a carved stone capital of medieval date, showing two acrobats,
a favoured theme in Gill's own sculpture (see also *cats* 59 and
60).

59 Acrobats on a Stage
mid-1920s
Pencil and red and blue ink
6 × 5½ in / 15.2 × 14 cm
Inscr: EG
The Trustees of the British Museum

Gill's diaries contain many sketches in the margins, depicting himself and his wife Ethel Mary engaged in sexual intercourse while adopting a variety of acrobatic poses. This design of naked tumblers is similar to many of these drawings; they also could be in the act of copulation.

60 Naked Acrobats
mid-1920s
Pencil and coloured wash
9 × 7 in / 22.9 × 17.8 cm
Inscr: *Man is matter and spirit — both real & both good*
The Trustees of the British Museum

One of Gill's great credos was the phrase written along the bottom of this drawing. It forms the last sentence of his preface or 'Apology' to his collection of essays entitled *Art-Nonsense and Other Essays*, published in 1929. The composition looks as though it was inspired by a medieval stone capital depicting acrobats.

61 Small Female Torso
1924
Hoptonwood stone relief on rosewood base
4½ × 3¾ × 1⅛ in / 11.5 × 9.5 × 2.8 cm
Inscr: for ELIZh. June 1 1924 on verso
Art Collection, Harry Ransom Humanities Research Center, The University of Texas at Austin (897)

The birthday of Gill's eldest daughter, Elizabeth, was 1 June. In 1924 she would have been nineteen. The inscription on this work reveals that it was probably a present for her birthday; perhaps she also posed for the work. Gill introduced the theme of the naked female torso into his work in 1920 (see cat.42). See ill. p.55

62 Deposition

1924
Black marble, 30 × 12 × 8 in / 76.2 × 30.5 × 20.3 cm
Exh: Goupil Gallery Salon, Nov–Dec 1924 (462 at £70.0.0)
The King's School, Canterbury

Gill's diaries record for 12 September 1924: 'Began carving in
cellar workshop – Deposition, black marble'. Gill worked on
this sculpture from that date until 1 October, when he records
that he began rubbing and polishing it. From 2 to 4 October,
the work was polished, with Gill enlisting the help of Philip
Hagreen. When the polishing was finished on 4 October, Gill
made a stand for the work and photographed it (see below).
On 6 October he took it to the Goupil Gallery, London, to show
to William Marchant. It was then exhibited during November
and December in the Goupil Gallery's mixed Winter exhibition. Gill had worked in black marble only twice before; the
first time was in 1919, when he carved a crucifix for William
Marchant of the Goupil Gallery.
See p.62

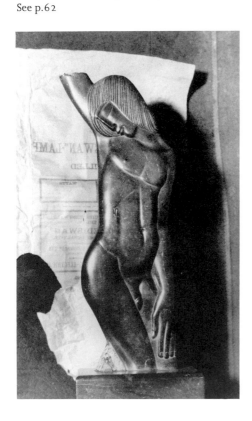

63 Design for Sculpture: Deposition

1923
Pencil, ink and crayon
4½ × 3¼ in / 11.4 × 8.2 cm
Inscr: *Descent from the Cross* (for black marble) EG.30.4.23
Art Collection, Harry Ransom Humanities Research Center,
The University of Texas at Austin (968[1])

The date on this drawing reveals that Gill had the idea for the
Deposition (cat.62) while still living at Ditchling, but only
carved it the following year, soon after moving to Capel-y-ffin.

64 Design for Sculpture: Deposition

1923
Pencil, ink and crayon
4¼ × 1¾ in / 10.8 × 4.4 cm
Art Collection, Harry Ransom Humanities Research Center,
The University of Texas at Austin (968[3])

65 Deposition

1924
Wood engraving, 4⅛ × 1½ in / 10.5 × 3.8 cm
City Museum and Art Gallery, Stoke-on-Trent

This wood engraving cut in 1924 [P289] keeps close in design
to the black marble carving of the same subject, which Gill
carved in September 1924 (cat.62). Gill also produced an
intaglio edition of the design.

Cat. 64   Cat. 65

66 Crucifixion

1925
Portland stone, with added colour
$89 \times 37\frac{3}{8} \times 3\frac{1}{8}$ in / $226 \times 95 \times 8$ cm
Exh: Goupil Gallery Salon, Nov–Dec 1925 (475 at £200.0.0)
Art Collection, Harry Ransom Humanities Research Center,
The University of Texas at Austin (898)

Gill's diaries record that he began carving a big crucifix on 8
June 1925. He worked on it regularly during June, and by 23
June he had finished working with the claw chisel on the sculpture. He began with the flat chisel on 1 July and then put the
work to one side until 17 September. He finished it on 5
October and on that same day began packing it for exhibition
in London. It was sent off on 7 October and shown at the
Goupil Gallery's Winter Salon. An entry for 25 January 1926
records that Gill went 'to Goupil and transferred Crucifix to
Westminster Cathedral'. It could well have been this work.
See ill. p.63

67 The Sleeping Christ

1925
Caen stone on ebony base
$12 \times 17 \times 3\frac{3}{4}$ in / $30.5 \times 43.2 \times 8.8$ cm
Manchester City Art Galleries

Christ sleeps at peace with his head resting on his right hand,
and with his upper torso naked. Christ sleeping is not an
incident reported in the Gospels. Gill more usually depicts
Christ either crucified or as a man of action, driving the traders
from the Temple. In choosing to portray Christ in this way, Gill
renders Him tender and sensual. With his eyes closed, it gives
him a connection with heads of Buddha turned inward in
meditation. The stone Gill used was an odd unsquared piece
and he has chosen to leave the upper edge jagged, to emphasise
its materiality. The sculpture was bought from Gill in 1925 by
Charles Rutherston.
See ill. p.56

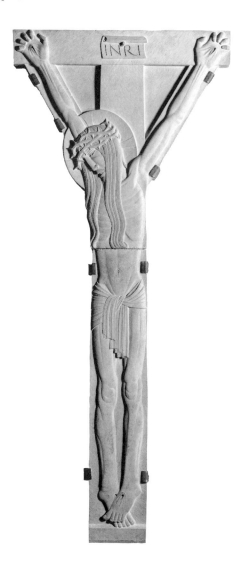

68 Rossall School War Memorial Altarpiece

1927
Oak relief
$36 \times 84 \times 2\frac{3}{8}$ in / 91.5 × 213.4 × 6 cm
Exh: Goupil Gallery Salon, Oct–Nov 1927 (248)
Rossall School, Fleetwood

Gill's letters reveal that he first heard of the possibility of being commissioned to make an oak altarpiece for the new War Memorial Chapel at Rossall School in December 1925, and he visited the school on 18 December to look at the site. The subject proposed then was the Adoration of the Three Kings. Rossall School had three advisers from the art world who were responsible for commissioning the architect Sir Robert Lorimer to build the chapel. The three men were Sir Charles Holmes, Director of the National Gallery, Sir Edwin Lutyens, architect, and Charles Rutherston, collector. Rutherston is believed to have proposed Gill as the sculptor for the chapel's altarpiece, although Sir Robert Lorimer did not want him. In January 1926 Gill produced a design for the altar and in April he sent off a full-size drawing to the school. In June he produced a second design and during August and early September executed a second full-size drawing, which was dispatched to the school on 7 September. In October this drawing was shown at the Goupil Gallery Autumn Salon, where it was highly praised, and the commission was finally secured. On 19 January 1927 the wooden panels for the altar arrived at Gill's studio from a supplier in Edinburgh and he began to trace the drawing onto them. This task took until 22 January (see cat.70). In March, while Gill was in France, his assistant Laurie Cribb began cutting out the background. Gill began to carve the altarpiece on 4 July and worked on it until 2 September when he packed it ready for dispatch to London the following day. He continued to work on it in London between 7 and 13 September and then exhibited it at the Goupil Gallery Autumn Salon during October and November. On 9 March 1928 Gill visited Rossall School to see the altarpiece fixed in place in the War Memorial Chapel. ¶A soldier in a tin hat of the type worn during the First World War kneels at the right of the Cross. Gill employs this device in three other works, firstly on his Trumpington Cross War Memorial, Cambridge, 1923, then in the wood-engraved scene of *The Kiss of Judas*, from *Passio Domini Nostri Jesu Christi*, published in 1926, and thirdly in the carved relief of *St Martin of Tours*, at Campion Hall, Oxford, 1936.
See ill. p.59

69 Design for Sculpture: Rossall School War Memorial Altarpiece

1925
Pencil
$2\frac{1}{2} \times 5$ in / 6.5 × 12.7 cm
Rossall School, Fleetwood

This small rough pencil sketch was probably done on the occasion of Gill's visit to the school in December 1925 to consider the commission.

Cat.68, details

70 Designs for Sculpture:
Rossall School War Memorial Altarpiece
1927
a. Left-hand side of central panel
Pencil on paper, 34 × 18 in / 87 × 46 cm
b. Right-hand side of central panel
Pencil on paper, 34 × 18 in / 87 × 45.7 cm
Inscr: EG.22.1.27 top left
Courtesy of David Mayou

These are full-scale drawings for two sections of the altarpiece
that Gill carved for Rossall School (see cat.68). The drawings
show the two thieves at Christ's crucifixion, one facing towards
Christ and the other turned away.

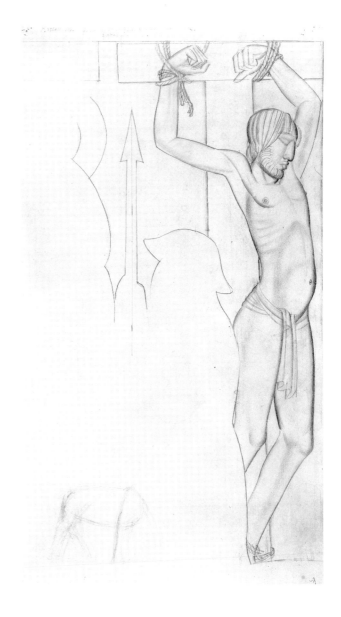

71 Tobias and Sara

1926
Portland stone
18½ × 23 × 4½ in / 46.9 × 58.4 × 11.4 cm
Exh: Goupil Gallery Salon, Oct–Nov 1926 (489 at £70.0.0)
The President and Fellows of St John's College, Oxford

On 4 September 1926 Gill began a stone carving with a work-ing title of 'Lovers with arms round necks'. After nine days' work he finished the sculpture in the afternoon of 15 Septem-ber and then christened it 'Tobias and Sara'. These two figures appear in the Book of Tobit, an Apocryphal book. The book concerns Tobit, a pious Jew who became poor and blind. He remembered a debt due from an old friend and he sent his son Tobias, along with a companion, to recover it. The companion revealed himself as the angel Raphael and he helped to rescue a kinswoman, Sara, from the power of a demon Asmodaeus who had killed her seven husbands before the marriages were consummated. Tobias then married Sara, who was 'sensible, brave and very beautiful' (Tobit, 6, v.12). Raphael recovered the debt and helped Tobias to heal Tobit of his blindness. Gill had produced engravings for 'The Song of Songs' in 1925 and the two figure types of Tobias and Sara are very close to the naked pairs of lovers who populate the engravings for this book, although Tobias does not sport a beard. Gill rounds off the left-hand edge of the stone relief with a suggestion of furniture, upon which Sara rests her arm. The right-hand edge is left rough.
See ill. p.57

72 Mary Magdalen

1926
Caen stone relief, with added colour
13 × 13 × 3 in / 33.1 × 33.1 × 7.6 cm
Inscr: EG
Exh: Goupil Gallery Salon, Oct–Nov 1926 (490 at £25.0.0)
John Schroder

Mary Magdalen, a sinner and a follower of Christ, is depicted with her box of ointment, which she used to anoint his feet. Her right hand holds the box, while her left presses her long hair, which she used to dry Christ's feet (Gospel of St Luke, 7, v.37). The design of the relief is similar to the upper half of a wood engraving of St Mary Magdalen, executed in 1926 for *Passio Domini Nostri Jesu Christi*, published by the Golden Cockerel Press in 1926 [P349]. In the wood engraving Mary Magdalen pours the ointment onto the head of Christ, who appears below her, attended by two apostles. Gill worked on this relief from 15 to 21 September, beginning it in the evening of the day he finished working on the sculpture *Tobias and Sara* (cat.71).
See ill. below

73 Rubbing of Sculpture: Mary Magdalen

1926
Wax crayon on paper
14 × 14 in / 35.6 × 35.6 cm
Inscr: *Rubbing of Incised line in stone before carving EG Sept 26*
Private collection

74 Stele

1927
Hoptonwood stone double relief
$66\frac{7}{8} \times 22\frac{1}{4} \times 3\frac{1}{2}$ in / 170 × 56.5 × 9 cm
Exh : Goupil Gallery, March 1928 (2)
Trustees of the late Oliver Lodge by courtesy of
Gloucester City Museums

Oliver Lodge was a good friend of Gill, and when Lodge's first
wife Wynlane died in 1922, he commissioned a headstone
from the artist. In March 1923 Gill carved a slate headstone
with the subject of a mother and child in memory of Wynlane
Lodge and this was placed in St Michael's churchyard,
Wilsford, near Amesbury, Wiltshire. Gill's diary for 11 July
1927 records 'Oliver Lodge gravestone sketch' and it appears
that Lodge commissioned a second headstone from Gill with
no obvious commemorative purpose. When it was executed
Lodge did not want it sited in a churchyard because he 'feared
the weather would damage the beautiful polish of the carving'.
Lodge placed it on loan with the Tate Gallery in 1928 and it
remained there until 1967 when it was transferred to Gloucester City Museums. Lodge died in 1955.

75 Design for Sculpture : Double Headstone for Alice Jameson

1933
Pencil and watercolour
$15 \times 10\frac{1}{2}$ in / 38.1 × 26.7 cm
Inscr : EG 20.2.33
P. G. H. Wilson

This design is for a headstone of Portland stone which Gill
carved in memory of Alice Jameson (1899–1932). He received
the commission from the widower, Captain Jameson, in the
Spring of 1932 and on 9 and 10 April Gill drew designs for
a headstone. He then drew this design in February 1933, and
a further drawing for the project was executed on 2 May 1933.
The headstone was rejected by the cemetery authorities as
being inappropriate because of its nudity. Its present
whereabouts are unknown.
¶Gill was fond of this type of headstone, making a version for
Oliver Lodge in 1927 (cat.74) and a further uncommissioned
example, which he exhibited at the RA Summer Exhibition in
1939, under the title *Memento Mori*.

76 Mankind

1927–8
Hoptonwood stone
95 × 24 × 18 in / 241.3 × 61 × 45.7 cm
Exh : Goupil Gallery, March 1928 (1)
Tate Gallery

Gill had purchased a large piece of Hoptonwood stone while
he lived at Ditchling. In 1924 when he moved to Capel-y-ffin,
the stone was left at Ditchling. In the Autumn of 1927, in
preparation for his forthcoming solo exhibition at the Goupil
Gallery in March 1928, Gill took a studio in Glebe Place, Chelsea, and on 13 September the large piece of Hoptonwood stone
arrived from Ditchling. On 29 October Gill began to carve
Mankind from it. He worked on *Mankind* throughout November, December and until 24 January 1928. It was the most cele-
brated sculpture in his Goupil Gallery exhibition and was
bought from the show by the sculptor Eric Kennington for
£800, although it was actually priced at 1000 guineas.
¶In 1938 Kennington and Julian Huxley offered *Mankind* to
Whipsnade Zoo as a perfect specimen of humankind. The
Council of the Zoo rejected it on the grounds that only sculpture of naked animals, not humans, would be appropriate for
them. It was then offered by Kennington to the Tate Gallery.
The British Council sent it to New York as part of their con-
tribution for the 1939 World Fair. The outbreak of the Second
World War prevented its immediate return and it was shown
at the Museum of Modern Art, New York, from 1939 to 1943
and then at the Art Gallery of Toronto between March 1943
and December 1945.
See ill. p.61

77 Self-Portrait

1927
Wood engraving, $6\frac{7}{8} \times 4\frac{3}{4}$ in / 17.5 × 12 cm
Private collection

Gill made a self-portrait drawing on 20 December 1927. He
transferred the design onto a wood block on 23 December and
then produced this wood engraving on 27 and 28 December
[P497]. The image was used as the frontispiece to Douglas
Cleverdon's book *Engravings by Eric Gill : A Selection*, Bristol
1929. Gill is here wearing a paper hat traditionally worn by
stone-masons. He was aged forty-five when he engraved this.

78 Adam

1927–8
Bath stone
$28\frac{3}{8} \times 6\frac{1}{4} \times 5\frac{7}{8}$ in / 72 × 16 × 15 cm
Inscr: EG on verso of base
Exh: Goupil Gallery, March 1928 (7)
Art Collection, Harry Ransom Humanities Research Center,
The University of Texas at Austin (899)

Gill began work on *Adam* on 19 November 1927, having
already started a companion sculpture of *Eve* (collection Tate
Gallery) on 2 November. Both are carved from Bath stone, are
similar in size and were executed in conjunction with *Mankind*
(*cat.76*). *Adam* was finished on 9 February 1928. Sir Hugh
Walpole, the collector, purchased the work from the Goupil
Gallery exhibition. Gill utilised the pose of Adam, with his
arms over his head, in two other works of similar date, the
large wooden *Caryatid*, 1927, and a second version of *St
Sebastian*, 1927 (also see *cat.38*).
See ill. p.60

79 Headdress

1928
Beer stone, with added colour
32 × 8 × 3 in / 81.3 × 20.3 × 7.6 cm
Exh: Goupil Gallery, March 1928 (11)
Private collection

Headdress was carved between 20 and 26 February 1928, a total
of seven days' work, and was made ready just in time for Gill's
solo exhibition at the Goupil Gallery in March 1928. The work
was bought by Sir Edward Maufe, who displayed it in a special
niche in the dining room of his home at Shepherds Hill, Bux-
ted, Sussex. This exotic female nude with her decorative mane
of hair and two necklaces is a confident development from the
first sensual nude that Gill carved in 1910 (*cat.4*).

80 Model for Sculpture: The East Wind

1929
Bath stone relief
10 × 27¾ × 4 in / 25.6 × 70.5 × 10.2 cm
Exh: Goupil Gallery Salon, Nov 1929 (193 at £100)
Tate Gallery

In January 1928 Gill received a commission from Charles
Holden to carve three stone reliefs of figures of Winds for the
exterior decoration of the new London Underground Railway
Headquarters at 55 Broadway. Gill led a team of five other
sculptors, Eric Aumonier, A. H. Gerrard, Henry Moore, Samuel
Rabinovitch and Allan Wyon, each of whom carved one Wind,
making a total of eight. There were two Winds for each cardinal point; the East Wind was represented by male figures,
the West Wind by female figures, while the North and South
Winds were represented by both male and female figures. Gill
carved his three full-scale Winds, the East, the North and the
South, on site at 55 Broadway between November 1928 and
February 1929. This model is one-quarter of the size of the
panel on the London Underground building. Although Gill's
diaries reveal that he made preliminary models in November
1928 before carving his panels *in situ*, this stone relief was
carved between 21 and 26 October 1929, long after the work
on 55 Broadway was finished. It appears to have been made
for exhibition at the Goupil Gallery. The Tate Gallery bought
this model from the Goupil Gallery show (see also *cat.*81).

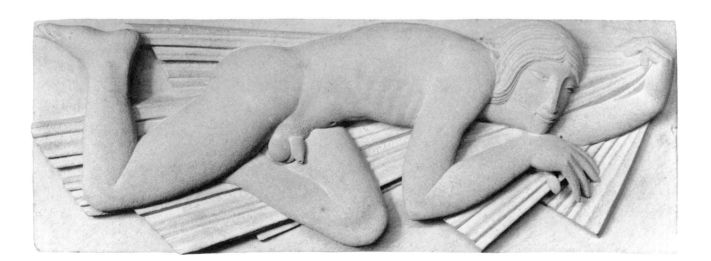

81 Model for Sculpture: The North Wind

1929
Bath stone relief
$10 \times 27\frac{3}{4} \times 4$ in / $25.6 \times 69.8 \times 10.2$ cm
Tate Gallery

Although Gill's diary for October 1929 only records the carving of the smaller versions of *The East Wind* (cat.80) and *The South Wind* (present whereabouts unknown, but reproduced in *Studio* vol.100, July–Dec 1930, p.231), it seems likely that this relief was carved at the same time.

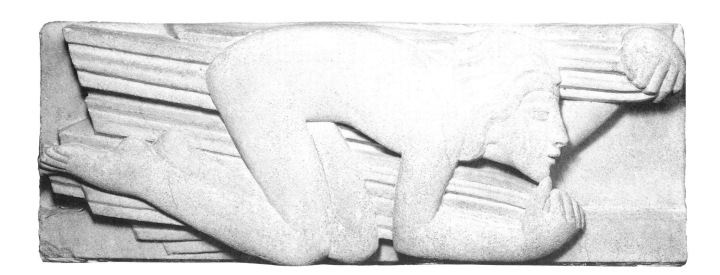

82 Model for Sculpture: The Sower

1931
Bath stone
$56\frac{1}{2} \times 18\frac{1}{2} \times 6\frac{1}{2}$ in / 143.5 × 47 × 16.5 cm
Exh: French Gallery, Nov 1933 (2 at £100)
Manchester City Art Galleries (represented by photographs)

In October 1929 Gill received a commission to provide sculptures for Broadcasting House, the new headquarters of the BBC, via the art critic Herbert Read. The Directors of the BBC asked for a sculpture of a man 'Broadcasting' to be set in the entrance hall of Broadcasting House. Gill wrote to his brother Cecil: 'Comic thought, when you consider the quality of BBC semination, to compare it with the efforts of a simple countryman sewing corn'. Gill drew designs for *The Sower* on 13 April 1931 (see *cat*.83), on 11 June (see *cat*.84), and further designs on 6 and 7 August. He began carving this half-size model on 15 August and had probably finished it by 24 August, the date on which he started carving the BBC sculptures on site at Broadcasting House. In October 1933, just before the opening of his solo exhibition at the French Gallery, Gill spent four days, 20, 25, 28 and 29 October, working on this model. It was bought by Charles Rutherston who presented it to the City Art Gallery, Manchester.

83 Design for Sculpture: The Sower

1931
Pencil and orange crayon
$12\frac{1}{2} \times 9$ in / 31.9 × 22.9 cm
Inscr: *Eric G / EG 13.4.31 / Ariel Broadcasting / Scale 1″ — 1′ 0″ / (Proposed Carving in Entrance Hall, Broadcasting House / Tree in low relief on background / figure of Sower in high relief)*
Private collection

This drawing shows that Gill originally proposed the figure of the Sower as a younger man whose right hand was held aloft, presumably after scattering seeds. An alternative sketch of the figure with his right hand dipped into a seed bag is included on this sheet of paper. When the sculpture was carved full-size on site in January 1932, the pose of the alternative figure was adopted. The low relief tree was rejected. This drawing was originally owned by Sir Edward Maufe.

84 Design for Sculpture: The Sower

1931
Pencil squared for transfer, $14\frac{1}{2} \times 10$ in / 36.8 × 25.4 cm
Inscr: *Eric G 11.6.31*
The Chairman and Board of Governors of the BBC

This drawing depicts a naked male figure holding an open bowl in his left arm, with his right hand dipped into it. The male figure bears a strong resemblance to Leslie French, who posed naked to Gill several times in 1931 for preparatory drawings for the *Ariel* reliefs, which were also for the BBC (see *cats* 87–90).

85 Model for Sculpture: Prospero and Ariel

1931
Caen stone
$50 \times 18 \times 14$ in / 127 × 45.7 × 35.6 cm
Exh: Leicester Galleries, April 1935 (175)
Tate Gallery

This is also part of the commission for the BBC (see *cat*.82). The BBC asked for a group depicting Prospero and Ariel, characters from Shakespeare's *The Tempest*, to be set above the main door. Gill produced drawings showing two variants of the group and executed both designs as models in stone between 4 May and 15 August 1931. The Tate Gallery's *Prospero and Ariel* group shows Prospero with a shorter beard, and Ariel as a younger child. This is the design that was carved full-size, and the Tate Gallery's model is one-third of the size. The other version, which Gill later titled *Abraham and Isaac*, has the beard of the older figure reaching down to the top of the smaller figure. Gill showed the *Abraham and Isaac* group at the French Gallery in November 1936, and it was sold to a private collector in New York in December 1938. Its present whereabouts are unknown. The Tate Gallery bought this model of *Prospero and Ariel* from the Leicester Galleries in October 1935. Although the BBC believed that Gill had produced for them a group depicting Prospero and Ariel, Gill introduced stigmata to Ariel's hands, thus giving the work a spiritual dimension; Gill explained: 'In my view the figures at Broadcasting House are as much God the Father and God the Son as they are Shakespeare's characters'.
See ill. p.64

Top part of *Prospero and Ariel*
being winched into place at the BBC
1932

86 Design for Sculpture: Prospero and Ariel

1931
Pencil, $12 \times 6\frac{1}{2}$ in / 30.5 × 16.5 cm
Inscr: *Main Entrance (tracing of no 2)*
Private collection

87 Model for Sculpture:
Ariel Piping to the Children
1931
Bath stone relief
$16 \times 26\frac{3}{8} \times 3\frac{1}{8}$ in / $40.6 \times 67 \times 8$ cm
Exh: Royal Scottish Academy Summer Exhibition, Edinburgh,
1935 (70)
Art Collection, Harry Ransom Humanities Research Center,
The University of Texas at Austin (901)

Gill was asked by the BBC to provide three stone relief panels
of Ariel and other figures to be sited above the three doors,
excluding the main door, which give access to Broadcasting
House. This is one of two models for a larger relief of the same
subject which is set above a door on the Langham Street side,
the east side, of Broadcasting House. The full-size panels are
four feet by six feet, so this model is about one-third of full
size. The theme of the relief does not come specifically from
The Tempest, but is thought to relate to the BBC Children's
Hour. Gill had two ideas for the layout of the relief; either Ariel
could lead a group of children, or he could sit in their midst
providing music for them. This model shows the latter idea,
which is the one that was executed. However, when Gill carved
the stone panel on the BBC he only placed one child either side
of Ariel instead of three as here. This model was carved
between 3 July and October 1931 (see also *cat.*88). There is
an incised design for the same subject carved on the back of
this stone.
See ill. p.6

88 Design for Sculpture:
Ariel Piping to the Children
1931
Pencil on tracing paper
5×7 in / 12.7×17.8 cm
Inscr: *Eric G / Tracing of design No.3 Ariel and Children
5.8.31* – along bottom edge
Collection of Richard Ayre and Guy Burch

By August 1931 Gill had refined his idea for the relief of *Ariel
Piping to the Children* down to this design, with two children
dancing either side of Ariel, who no longer sits but joins them
in the music. This drawing was made on 5 August and the
model based on it was begun on 19 August. Its present
whereabouts are unknown; it is reproduced in the *Illustrated
London News*, 3 October 1931, p.519.

89 Model for Sculpture: Ariel Between Wisdom and Gaiety

1931
Bath stone relief
$16 \times 27 \times 3\frac{1}{2}$ in / $40.6 \times 68.6 \times 8.9$ cm
The Chairman and Board of Governors of the BBC

This is the model for a relief panel of the same subject and composition which is set above a door on the Portland Place side of Broadcasting House. It is about one-third of full size. The source of the subject is not found in *The Tempest* and must have stemmed from the BBC. The inspiration for the composition is taken from the tomb of Mary of Anjou in Naples, where Mary is borne aloft by two supporting angels. Gill retains the feathered wings for his two figures personifying Wisdom and Gaiety. The full-size relief was the first of the three *Ariel* reliefs to be started on site at the BBC. Gill drew out the design onto the panel on site at the BBC on 27 May 1931, so this model must have been executed prior to that date.

90 Model for Sculpture: Ariel Hearing Celestial Music

1931
Bath stone relief
$16 \times 27 \times 3\frac{1}{2}$ in / $40.6 \times 68.6 \times 8.9$ cm
The Chairman and Board of Governors of the BBC

This is the model for a relief panel of the same subject and composition which is placed above a door on the Portland Place side of Broadcasting House. It is about one-third of full size. The source of the subject is not found in *The Tempest* and must, like cat.89, have stemmed from the BBC. This relief keeps close in its design to that of *Ariel Between Wisdom and Gaiety*, with the two supporting angelic figures very similar in both, with only modifications in their arm positions.

Gill carving *Ariel Between Wisdom and Gaiety*
1931
See cat.89

91 La Belle Sauvage

1932
Bath stone high relief
$19 \times 8\frac{1}{2} \times 3\frac{1}{2}$ in / $48.3 \times 21.6 \times 8.9$ cm
Exh: French Gallery, Nov 1933 (4 at £45)
Art Collection, Harry Ransom Humanities Research Center,
The University of Texas at Austin (903)

On 5 November 1928 Gill drew a design of a female nude
standing in foliage, for a sculpture commissioned by Leonard
Woolf. He carved the design in marble in relief form in
September 1930 and then showed the work at the Goupil
Gallery Salon in November 1931. The drawing marked the first
appearance of Gill's 'Belle Sauvage' theme, which was used for
two sculptures and four wood engravings (see cat.92). This is
the second of the sculptures and it was begun on 22 November
1932. Gill's diary records that he carved it for Rex Nan Kivell
of the Redfern Gallery but it ended up in the possession of
Beatrice Warde, typographic consultant to the Monotype Cor-
poration. Although the female figure appears at first glance to
be pagan and sensual, she nevertheless raises her left hand in
blessing. Before sending this stone to the exhibition at the
French Gallery in November 1933, Gill worked on it on 29 and
30 September and 1 and 21 October.
See ill. facing title page

92 La Belle Sauvage: Girl Standing

1929
Wood engraving, $3 \times 2\frac{3}{4}$ in / 7.6×6 cm
City Museum and Art Gallery, Stoke-on-Trent

Gill cut this wood engraving in 1929 [P606] as a design for
Cassell & Co Ltd, and it was used on the title page of his *Art-
Nonsense and Other Essays*, 1929, published by Cassell & Co Ltd
& Francis Walterson. The black figure version was used for the
title page of the large paper edition of *Art-Nonsense and Other
Essays* (see also cat.91).

93 Odysseus Welcomed from the Sea by Nausicaa
1933
Polished Portland stone relief
$10\frac{1}{2} \times 16 \times 1$ ft / $317 \times 491.5 \times 39.5$ cm
Inscr: THERE IS GOOD HOPE THAT THOU MAYEST SEE THY FRIENDS
HOMER / ODY. Eric G, and NAUSIKAA and OΔYSSEUS
Midland Hotel, Morecambe

Gill had a meeting with Oliver Hill, architect of the new Midland Hotel, Morecambe, on 8 August 1932. The hotel had been commissioned from Hill by the London, Midland and Scottish Railway. On 16 August Gill made a drawing for a relief panel for the dining room of the hotel (see cat.94). He made a second drawing for the relief on 18 November (see cat.95). After a meeting with the LMS Directors on 30 January 1933, Gill produced a third design for the relief panel on 19 and 20 February (see cat.96). On 12 March Gill recorded in his diary: 'Experimental carving in polished Portland [stone]', thus the material for the hotel relief must have been decided upon by that date. Gill carved the relief on site in the lounge of the hotel, with the help of Laurie Cribb and Donald Potter, between 11 May and 27 June 1933. Gill attended the lunch to celebrate the opening of the Midland Hotel on 12 July 1933. He had made a drawing in July 1932 of two naked males frolicking in the sea with three naked females and gave this the title of 'High Jinks in Paradise'. It was reproduced in *Architec-*

tural Review, vol.75, May 1934, p.162, with the caption stating that it was the first design for the Midland Hotel relief. The LMS Directors probably would not have accepted pagan nudity as a decorative feature in their new hotel and Gill altered the subject to an incident from the life of Odysseus, which symbolised hospitality. The story comes from Homer's *Odyssey*; Nausicaa was the daughter of King Alcinous of Phaeacia. She found Odysseus shipwrecked on the coast, fed and clothed him and brought him to her father's court. Gill depicts Odysseus stepping from the sea and taking the hand of Nausicaa. She is accompanied by three female attendants, who carry food, drink and clothing. Odysseus is presumably naked as he steps from the sea, but he carries a convenient branch which conceals his genitals. In a letter to G.K.Chesterton on the subject of this relief, written on 25 May 1933, Gill remarked: 'Incidentally it is what is technically called a "holy picture" – but the LMS don't know that'.

94 Design for Sculpture:
Odysseus Welcomed from the Sea by Nausicaa
1932
Pencil, $9\frac{1}{2} \times 11\frac{1}{2}$ in / 24 × 29.2 cm
Inscr: *Morecambe Bay Hotel, Dining-room carved [?] panel, 1″ relief. EG 16.8.32 and for Leonard W. Eric G*
Art Collection, Harry Ransom Humanities Research Center,
The University of Texas at Austin (1076)

This pencil drawing for the carved relief in the lounge of the Midland Hotel, Morecambe (cat.93) is 1/24th in scale.

95 Design for Sculpture:
Odysseus Welcomed from the Sea by Nausicaa
1932
Pencil, $6\frac{3}{4} \times 10\frac{1}{4}$ in / 17 × 26 cm
Inscr: *Morecambe Bay Hotel, lounge panel..EG 18 Nov.'32*
Art Collection, Harry Ransom Humanities Research Center,
The University of Texas at Austin (1077[1])

This is the second design for the carved relief in the Midland Hotel (see also cat.94), and this too is 1/24th in scale.

96 Design for Sculpture:
Odysseus Welcomed from the Sea by Nausicaa
1933
Pencil, $9\frac{3}{4} \times 12\frac{1}{8}$ in / 24.8 × 30.8 cm
Inscr: *Morecambe Bay L.M.S. Hotel Odyssey vii- line 78 or thereabouts. EG 20.2.'33 and for Leonard Woolf*
Art Collection, Harry Ransom Humanities Research Center,
The University of Texas at Austin (1078[2])

See also cats 93, 94 and 95.

Cat.94

97 Design for Mosaic for Ceiling of Midland Hotel, Morecambe

1933
Pencil and watercolour
9 in / 22.9 cm diameter
Inscr : *Morecambe ceiling 25.3.33 EG.*
Fiona MacCarthy

Gill also received a commission from the LMS Railway via Oliver Hill to carve two sea-horses for the exterior front of the Midland Hotel, to incise a map of the area onto the wall of the bar, and to design a mosaic for the ceiling of the large circular staircase, one of the main architectural features of the hotel. The chosen subject of Neptune and Triton was taken from Greek mythology, presumably to create a link with the carved relief of Odysseus (see *cat.*93). This drawing was executed on 25 March 1933 and depicts Neptune crowned and seated on a throne attended by two mermaids. On 5 April Gill made a second design for the ceiling (see *cat.*98). He drew the design in colour directly onto the ceiling of the hotel between 1 and 24 May. It was not translated into mosaic, and remains today as he left it.

Ceiling decoration as executed

98 Design for Mosaic for Ceiling of Midland Hotel, Morecambe

1933
Pencil and watercolour
10½ in / 26.7 cm diameter
Inscr : *Morecambe, L.M.S. hotel, proposed mosaic on staircase ceiling 1 / 16 full size.. EG 5.4.'32 ;*
Neptune shd. hold trident.. 10ft.circle ¼″ up ; AND.HEAR.OLD. TRITON.BLOW. HIS.WREATHED.HORN
Sheffield City Art Galleries

This drawing, the second made for the Midland Hotel staircase ceiling decoration (see *cat.*97), is closest to the design as executed. Gill has written the date of 5 April 1932 on this sheet, but it was actually drawn on 5 April 1933. The drawing shows Neptune crowned and seated on a throne, attended by two mermaids to his right. To his left, emerging from the sea, is his son Triton, who holds a trident. Triton is usually depicted with a horn or shell, instead of a trident, which is Neptune's symbol. When Gill drew the design on the ceiling, he replaced Triton's trident with a horn. In both this design and the ceiling decoration, Gill has given Neptune stigmata in his hands and feet, thereby alluding to the figure of the crucified Christ. He called his relief of Odysseus and Nausicaa a 'holy picture' (see *cat.*93), and he has converted this into one also. This drawing was given to the Graves Art Gallery, Sheffield by the Sheffield Print Club in 1936.

99 Adam and Eve Garden Roller

c. 1933–4
Portland stone and iron
28 in / 71 cm total length
15¾ in / 40 cm diameter of roller
Leeds City Art Galleries

The letter-cutter David Kindersley was apprenticed to Gill in
1933. He recalled that the sides of this roller were carved by
him when he first worked with Gill: 'Of course he had a great
hand in the drawing on the roller for me to carve the boy and
girl. Incidentally he and I never thought of calling it *Adam and
Eve*! The stone was Portland and it was masoned from a very
rough lump and took a lot of doing and I shall never forget
it, it taught me the beginnings of stone carving. No drawings
were made except directly on to the stone ... The roller was
used on the tennis court at Pigotts and indeed apart from learning how to work stone, that was its main purpose.' As early
as 1915, Gill was commissioned to make carved garden rollers
for Sir Hugh Lane and Hilary Pepler.

100 Design for Sculpture:
League of Nations Creation Relief
1935
Pencil and red crayon
$9\frac{3}{4} \times 17\frac{3}{4}$ in / 24.8 × 45.1 cm
Inscr: 6 July 1935 Fr. D'Arcy wants this
Campion Hall, Oxford

Gill met C. L. Stocks, a Commissioner of Crown Lands and an agent for the Foreign Office, on 30 January 1935 to discuss a commission for a large carved relief for the Assembly Hall of the new League of Nations building at Geneva. The relief would be a gift from the British Government to the League of Nations. Christian subject-matter, such as the Good Samaritan, had been considered, but was thought too narrow for the numerous religions represented at the League of Nations. After mischievously proposing the subject of 'Christ Driving out the Money Changers from the Temple', Gill then devised a scheme in which the central panel represents the 're-creation of man' by God, with the inscription 'Quid est homo, quod memor es ejus? Ad imaginem Dei creavit illum' (Genesis, 1, v.27); and underneath this some words from Gerard Manley Hopkins's 'The Wreck of the Deutschland': 'God mastering me, giver of breath and bread, world's strand sway of the sea, Lord of living and dead, over again I feel thy finger and find thee'. This central panel was about eight feet by thirty feet. The left-hand panel

'represents man's gifts to God (that is ourselves, as we have nothing else to give)'; and the right-hand panel shows 'God's gifts to man, that is the whole created world'. Gill received the formal commission from Parliament on 27 April 1935 and all the work was finished and in its place by August 1938. This drawing depicts on a small scale Gill's vast conception. It was owned by Father Martin d'Arcy, SJ, the author of numerous books on religion, who was appointed the Master of Campion Hall in 1934.

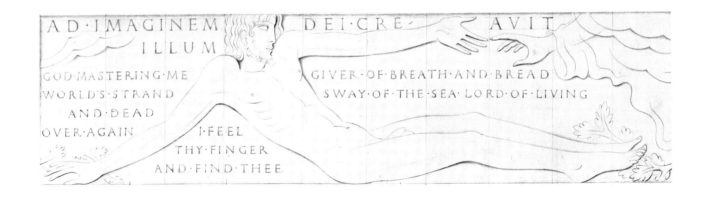

101 Design for Sculpture:
Altarpiece of the English Martyrs,
St George's Chapel, Westminster Cathedral
1939
Pencil and red ink, squared for transfer, 19⅞ × 14 in /
50.5 × 35.6 cm
Inscr: *W. Cath. St Georges Chapel (revised dr.)* ⅛ *full size*
EG 29.7.'39
Private collection

Shortly after Gill had finished his large relief for the League of
Nations in the late Summer of 1938, he was approached by the
Westminster Cathedral authorities and commissioned to carve
a stone altarpiece for St George's Chapel, the chapel of the
English Martyrs. He spent three days, 17 to 19 October 1938,
drawing designs for the altarpiece and then produced this
revised drawing in July 1939. He chose to portray St John
Fisher (1469–1535) and St Thomas More (1478–1535) on
either side of the Crucified Christ. Fisher and More, who were
friends, were executed for treason by Henry VIII. They were
canonised by the Catholic church in 1935. In Gill's design
More's pet monkey clings to his robes. Gill explained the inclu-
sion of this creature : 'St Thomas had a little Zoo of his own
at his house in Chelsea and among the inhabitants was a little
monkey of whom he was very fond. The sculptor has introduced the little animal as indicating by its very incongruity the
deeply human character of the Saint – so completely unlike the
conventional stained-glass figure. Moreover the animal does by
its caricature of humanity remind us of our lowly state.' The
altarpiece was not quite finished when Gill died in 1940, and
it remained in his workshop during the rest of the war. When
it was set in place in the cathedral in 1947, the monkey had
been removed from the carving. This was an act of philistine
vandalism, ordered by someone within ecclesiastical circles.
Since this drawing shows how the monkey took its part in the
design, it would be possible to use it to help reinstate the
animal.

102 Inscription: Night Treadeth on Day
1903
Ketton stone
8½ × 15 × 3½ in / 21.6 × 38.1 × 9 cm
Peter Nahum, London

The words are taken from the end of William Morris's poem
'The Wind's on the Wold', written in 1891 : 'Night treadeth
on day, / And for worst or best, / Right good is rest'. These
three lines were worked in embroidery by Morris's daughter
May as part of a tester hanging for Morris's four-poster bed.
The words are Morris's free translation of lines 86-7 of Book
x of Homer's *Odyssey*, in which Odysseus relates how night and
day intermingle in the land of the Laestrygons. The letters in
this relief stand out in relief form rather than being incised into
the stone, and Gill occasionally favoured this style of letter-
cutting during the years 1903–10. Relief letters can be found
on the *Crucifixion* panel of 1910 (*cat.*6). This stone is not listed
in Evan Gill's *Inventory of the Inscriptional Work of Eric Gill*, 1964,
even though its provenance was the artist's family. In his
'Inscriptions in stone', an Appendix to Edward Johnston's
seminal book of 1906, *Writing & Illuminating & Lettering*, Gill
advises that Ketton stone is 'only suitable for large lettering'.

Chronology

1882-1940

1882 22 February: Arthur Eric Rowton Gill born at Brighton, the second child and eldest son of twelve children of Arthur Tidman and Rose Gill. His father was Assistant Minister in a chapel of the Countess of Huntingdon's Connection.

1892 First surviving drawings, mainly of steam trains.

1897 Father joined Church of England and re-trained at Chichester Theological College. Family moved to Chichester. Attended Chichester Technical and Art School under tutelage of G. H. Catt.

1900 Apprenticed to William D. Caröe (1857–1938), architect to the Ecclesiastical Commissioners in Westminster. Worked at Caröe's office in Whitehall Place.

1903 Attended Westminster Technical Institute to learn stone-masonry and inscription cutting, and the Central School of Arts and Crafts where learned lettering from Edward Johnston. Left Caröe's office and received first professional commissions for inscriptions. Met Ethel Moore, daughter of the head verger of Chichester Cathedral.

Eric and Ethel's Wedding Day

1904 6 August: married Ethel at his father's church in Chichester. Set up home in flat in Battersea Bridge Buildings. Received commission from Count Harry Kessler of Weimar for engraved headings and titles.

1905 Joined Art Workers' Guild and Fabian Society. I June: birth of first daughter, Elizabeth (Betty). Taught monumental masonry and lettering for stone-masons at Paddington Institute. Moved to 20 Black Lion Lane, Hammersmith.

1906 Took on his first apprentice, Joseph Cribb. First visit to Rome. Began to make wood engravings. 18 August: birth of second daughter, Petra.

1907 Applied unsuccessfully for Principalship of Westminster Technical Institute. First visit to Chartres. II September: left London and moved to 'Sopers', Ditchling Village, Sussex.

1908 Resigned from the Art Workers' Guild and the Fabian Society. Befriended William Rothenstein, Ananda Coomaraswamy, Roger Fry and Jacob Epstein.

1909 Autumn: began figure sculpture and showed this new work to William Rothenstein, Roger Fry, Count Harry Kessler and Bernard Berenson.

1910 January: abortive attempt to study in Paris with the sculptor Maillol, arranged by Count Kessler. I February: birth of third daughter, Joanna. 15 June: attended inaugural meeting of the India Society. October: resigned from Paddington class in stone-masonry.

1911 January: first solo exhibition of figure carvings at Chenil Gallery, London. Contemporary Art Society purchased Crucifixion (cat.6) and A Roland for an Oliver (cat.4), reliefs from show. 24 August: Ethel had miscarriage and was unable to have more children as a result.

1912 Edward Johnston moved to Ditchling. Gill made sculptures and menu stands for Madame Strindberg's nightclub, The Cave of the Calf. October: exhibited five sculptures in Roger Fry's Second Post-Impressionist Exhibition.

1913 22 February: Eric and Ethel (now Mary) received into the Roman Catholic Church in Brighton. Spent the rest of the day walking the Downs with Leonard and Virginia Woolf. 16 August: received notice of commission for the Stations of the Cross for Westminster Cathedral (see cats 28–33). 13 November: moved from 'Sopers' to Hopkins Crank, north of Ditchling village.

1914 January: second solo exhibition, this time at Goupil Gallery, London. 8 April: gained the commission for the Stations of the Cross. First met André Raffalovich and Father John Gray. Exempted from war service in order to carve Westminster Cathedral Stations.

1915 April: received commission from Ernest Debenham to make village cross/war memorial for Bryantspuddle village, Dorset. Served on Mestrovic's Sculpture Exhibition committee at Victoria and Albert Museum. Asked to carve memorial for Nurse Edith Cavell for Trafalgar Square but did not accept.

1916 Hilary Pepler sets up printing press in Ditchling. Establishment of the magazine The Game. Carved font for St Joseph's Church at Pickering, Yorkshire. Designed war memorial for Civic Arts Association competition, with subject of 'Christ Driving out the Money Changers from the Temple' (see cats 45 and 46).

1917 Began negotiations for adoption of a son, Antonius Gordian. October: with Hilary Pepler discussed project for a religious order of artists with Father Vincent McNabb at Hawkesyard Priory, Staffordshire. Received commission from Michael Sadler to make war memorial for Leeds University (see cat.44).

1918 **7 January**: Gordian joined Gill family. **29 March**: **Good Friday** – canonical erection of Stations of the Cross, Westminster Cathedral. **April**: exhibition of drawings at Alpine Club Gallery. **3 June**: military exemption withdrawn. **29 July**: with Mary, Desmond Chute and Hilary Pepler invested as novices in Third Order of St Dominic. **September**: served as private in RAF Motor Transport division.

1919 **25 January**: with Hilary Pepler purchased Spoil Bank, Ditchling. **January**: visit to Hawkesyard Priory in company of Hilary Pepler and Stanley Spencer. Several commissions for war memorials; carved cross at Bisham, Berks. **August**: lecture tour in Ireland and Scotland with Pepler.

1920 Founder member of Society of Wood Engravers. Carved Chirk and South Harting War Memorials. Designed chapel for Ditchling Guild of St Joseph and St Dominic.

1921 David Jones came to Ditchling and Desmond Chute left to study for the priesthood. Began Stations of the Cross for St Cuthbert's Church, Bradford (*cat.34*), for his friend Father John O'Connor.

1922 Helped Father O'Connor with his translation of Jacques Maritain's *Art et Scholastique*, published in English in 1923. Began carving Leeds University War Memorial.

1923 **1 June**: Leeds University War Memorial dedicated and unveiled amid controversy. **October**: met Maritain in Paris

1924 Resigned from Guild of St Joseph and St Dominic, Ditchling. **January**: invited by HM Government to design 1d and 1½d stamps and designs for new silver coinage. **13 August**: left Ditchling, and the following day arrived at Capel-y-ffin, Wales.

1925 Turned down William Rothenstein's offer to teach at Royal College of Art. Met Stanley Morison and began to make designs for Perpetua typeface. Received commission for Rossall School War Memorial Altarpiece (*cat.68*). Publication of 'The Song of Songs', with EG engravings, by the Golden Cockerel Press. Arranged for William Marchant of the Goupil Gallery to be his sole agent. Carved Stations of the Cross for Church of Our Lady and St Peter, Leatherhead, Surrey. **Christmas**: pilgrimage to Rome.

1926 **May**: visited Salies-de-Béarn in foothills of Pyrenees. Met Jacques Maritain, Zadkine and Maillol in Paris. **November**: published *Id Quod Visum Placet*, sold out before publication.

1927 **February–April**: lived in Salies-de-Béarn. Elizabeth Gill married David Pepler, son of Hilary. **April**: first monograph on EG, written by John Rothenstein. **Autumn**: took studio in Glebe Place, Chelsea and carved several works there for forthcoming Goupil Gallery exhibition. Joint exhibition with David Jones at St George's Gallery. Publication of *Troilus and Criseyde* with EG engravings, by the Golden Cockerel Press. First designs for Gill Sans typeface.

1928 Befriended Henry Moore. **March**: solo exhibition at Goupil Gallery which was a critical and financial success. Received commission via Charles Holden for sculpture for London Underground Headquarters (see *cats 80 and 81*). **11 October**: left Capel y ffin and moved to Pigotts, near High Wycombe, Bucks. **20 November**: began carving London Underground *Winds* on site.

The quadrangle at Pigotts, with Stele (see cat. 74)

Gill in his Capel-y-ffin studio with Howard Coster

1929 Publication of *Art-Nonsense and Other Essays*, and *Engravings by Eric Gill: A Selection*, by Douglas Cleverdon. **6 August**: mother died in West Wittering. Publication of four volumes of Chaucer's *Canterbury Tales* by the Golden Cockerel Press. **October**: learnt via Herbert Read of the commission to make sculptures for the BBC's new building, Broadcasting House (see *cats* 82–90). Second monograph on EG's work, by Joseph Thorp.

1930 **January**: Petra Gill married Denis Tegetmeier, an engraver. **June**: visited Count Harry Kessler in Weimar. **July**: visited Salies-de-Béarn. **October–December**: nervous collapse, spent time in St John and St Elizabeth's Hospital, St John's Wood, London. **November**: Joanna (Joan) Gill married René Hague, a printer.

1931 **February**: began designs for BBC sculptures. **June**: began work on site at BBC on *Ariel* relief panels (see *cats* 85, 87, 89 and 90). Publication of *The Four Gospels* by the Golden Cockerel Press. Established his own press, Hague & Gill, at Pigotts.

1932 **January–August**: occupied with BBC carvings on site at Broadcasting House.

Gill climbing the scaffolding outside the BBC

1933 Founder member of Artists' International Association. Received commission for panels for new Archaeological Museum of Palestine, in Jerusalem. Publication of *Beauty Looks After Herself*. Carved relief for Midland Hotel, Morecambe (*cat.*93). **22 May**: death of his father in Brighton. **October**: carved crucifixion on St Thomas's Church, Hanwell, London, for Edward Maufe. **December**: exhibition of sculptures and engravings at the Goupil Gallery.

1934 Son-in-law David Pepler died. Travelled to Jerusalem to carve reliefs. Acquisition of a small stone sculpture by Henry Moore.

1935 Awarded Honorary Associateship of RIBA. Received commission for large carved relief for Assembly Hall of the League of Nations building, Geneva (*cat.*100).

1936 Appointed Royal Designer to Industry. Publication of *The Necessity of Belief*. Carved tombstone for his friend G.K.Chesterton.

1937 Awarded Honorary Associateship of Royal Society of British Sculptors. Elected Associate of the Royal Academy.

1938 Collaboration with boys of Blundell's School, Tiverton, Devon, on a new altar for their chapel. Awarded Honorary Doctorate of Law from Edinburgh University. Received commission from Westminster Cathedral for reredos for St George's Chapel (*cat.*101). **August**: League of Nations panel unveiled. Publication of *Twenty-five Nudes*. **October**: began designs for the Stations of the Cross for St Alban's Church, Oxford.

1939 Commission from Sir Edward Maufe to carve sculptures for new cathedral at Guildford. Building of church at Gorleston-on-Sea, near Great Yarmouth to Gill's design.

1940 Cancer of lung diagnosed. **April–July**: wrote *Autobiography*, published in December. **17 November**: died, buried in Speen Churchyard, with own designed headstone: 'Pray for Me / Eric Gill / Stone Carver 1882–1940'.

Select Bibliography

Gill's own writings

Eric Gill, *Art-Nonsense and Other Essays*, London, Cassell & Co
   & Francis Walterson, 1929
Eric Gill, *Autobiography*, London, Jonathan Cape, 1940 –
   reprinted by Lund Humphries Publishers, London, 1992
Ed. Walter Shewring, *The Letters of Eric Gill*, London, Jonathan Cape, 1947
Evan Gill, *Bibliography of Eric Gill*, London, Cassell & Co, 1953 –
   second edition, revised by D. Steven Cory and Julia MacKenzie,
   Winchester, St Paul Bibliographies, 1991

Gill's inscriptions and engravings

Evan Gill, *The Inscriptional Work of Eric Gill: An Inventory*, London, Cassell & Co, 1964
John Physick, *Catalogue of the Engraved Work of Eric Gill*, London,
   Victoria and Albert Museum, 1963
Christopher Skelton, *The Engravings of Eric Gill*, limited edition,
   Wellingborough, Skelton's Press, 1983 – unlimited edition by
   The Herbert Press, London, 1990

Gill's sculpture

J. K. M. Rothenstein, *Eric Gill*, London, Ernest Benn, 1927
Joseph Thorp, *Eric Gill*, London, Jonathan Cape, 1929

Gill's life and work

Robert Speaight, *The Life of Eric Gill*, London, Methuen & Co, 1966
Donald Attwatter, *A Cell of Good Living, The Life, Works and Opinions of Eric Gill*,
   London, Geoffrey Chapman, 1969
Malcolm Yorke, *Eric Gill: Man of Flesh and Spirit*, London, Constable, 1981
Fiona MacCarthy, *Eric Gill*, London, Faber and Faber, 1989

Lenders

Barbican Art Gallery gratefully acknowledges the support of the following lenders together with those who prefer to remain anonymous:

Austin, Art Collection, Harry Ransom Humanities Research Center, The University of Texas at Austin: cats. 1, 10, 11, 22, 36, 39, 42, 43, 49, 54, 55, 56, 57, 61, 63, 64, 66, 78, 87, 91, 94, 95, 96
Bury St Edmunds, P. G. H. Wilson: cat.75
Cambridge, Mr and Mrs Graham Howes: cat.23
Cambridge, The Provost and Scholars of King's College: cat.3
Canterbury, The King's School: cat.62
Cardiff, National Museum of Wales: cats 2, 19
Chichester, West Sussex Record Office, Eric Gill Collection: cats 16, 34, 35
Fleetwood, Rossall School: cats 68, 69
Gloucester, Trustees of the late Oliver Lodge by courtesy of Gloucester City Museums: cat.74
Hove Museum and Art Gallery: cat.48
The University of Hull Art Collection: cat.4
Leeds, City Art Galleries: cat.99
London, Victor Arwas: cat.15
London, Austin Desmond & Phipps: cat.5
London, Collection of Richard Ayre and Guy Burch: cat.88
London, The Chairman of the Board of Governors of the BBC: cats 84, 89, 90
London, The Bloomsbury Workshop: cats 29, 47, 50, 53
London, Ivor Braka Limited: cat.52
London, The Trustees of the British Museum: cats 8, 9, 24, 58, 59, 60
London, Faustus Fine Art, courtesy of David Mayou: cat. 70
London, The Fine Art Society plc: cats 25, 40
London, Stephen Keynes: cat. 21
London, Sandra Lummis Fine Art: cat.27
London, Peter Nahum: cat.102
London, The Tate Gallery: cats 6, 7, 18, 38, 76, 80, 81, 85
London, The Board of Trustees of the Victoria and Albert Museum: cats 30, 31, 32, 33
London, Douglas Woolf: cat.17
Manchester City Art Galleries: cats 13, 14, 28, 45, 46, 67, 82
Morecambe, Midland Hotel: cat.93
Oxford, Campion Hall: cat.100
Oxford, The President and Fellows of St John's College: cat.71
Sheffield, Fiona MacCarthy: cat.97
Sheffield City Art Galleries: cat.98
Somerset, John Schroder: cat.72
Stoke-on-Trent, City Museum and Art Gallery: cats 12, 20, 37, 41, 51, 65, 92

Photographic Acknowledgements

Barbican Art Gallery would like to extend sincere thanks to all lenders of works to the exhibition from both private and public collections who have kindly supplied photographic material for the catalogue or who have given permission for its use.

Our thanks must also be extended to:
The British Architectural Library/RIBA
The Henry Moore Centre for the Study of Sculpture, Leeds City Art Galleries
The Hulton-Deutsch Collection
Jonathan Morris-Ebbs, London
Norwin Photographic, Preston
John Skelton, Sussex